Now You Are a Missing Person

Now You Are a Missing Person

a memoir in poems, stories & fragments

by Susan Hayden

MOON
TIDE PRESS

~ 2023 ~

Now You Are a Missing Person
© Copyright 2023 Susan Hayden

Editor-in-chief
Eric Morago

Editor Emeritus
Michael Miller

Marketing Specialist
Ellen Webre

Proofreader
LeAnne Hunt

Front cover art
Hazel Angell

Author photo
Alexis Rhone Fancher

Book design
Michael Wada

Moon Tide logo design
Abraham Gomez

Now You Are a Missing Person
is published by Moon Tide Press

Moon Tide Press
6709 Washington Ave. #9297
Whittier, CA 90608
www.moontidepress.com

FIRST EDITION

Printed in the United States of America

ISBN # 978-1-957799-10-0

Praise for *Now You Are a Missing Person*

For many years, Susan Hayden has been the passionate, patient and loving den mother to the various scribes, tribes, loners, visionaries and rascals that make up the current poetry scene in Southern California. Her new collection of poems and other writings proves why she's so good at holding together these often disparate voices. It's because she is just as astute, powerful, funny, romantic, precise and driven as all the poets she has curated for. She is the reason that the fire of the written and spoken word in Southern California still burns as hot and wild as the hills in summertime.

—Dave Alvin

Imbued with the mercurial talents of the trickster and the poet, Susan Hayden weaves threads of verse and prose together for this hybrid memoir spanning her childhood, adolescence and adulthood. *Now You Are a Missing Person* pulls us into a San Fernando Valley suburb during a time when the reins on children (for better and worse) were not gripped so tightly. Through Hayden's lush and surprising language, we wind through suburban streets and board public buses that carry her to the dark and mysterious big city just on the other side of the interstate: Los Angeles. This story explores the concept of "outsiders" and "insiders." It challenges assumptions we hold about glamour, desire and even safety. Through its myriad journeying, the story moves us forward, even in its hybrid form, as we experience the main character transform into a woman searching for love and meaning. We see her flattened by grief, but this book is ultimately a testament that loss is not the end of love — and that in its place, new love, including a newfound self-love, can thrive.

—Cassandra Lane, *We Are Bridges*

Storytelling through poetry is one of the oldest, most rich forms of human communication. In Susan Hayden's stunning, genre-bending memoir, *Now You Are a Missing Person*, she explores a cultural and emotional lifetime in this tradition. "I was an anomaly in the West Valley," she writes "[A] trickster with a two-spirit nature, Technics turntable and a Barbie suitcase." These humorous and poignant lyrical narratives investigate a changing landscape: the explosive era of the 60s and 70s of California. We move with her beautiful voice and quick wit across time, through into the present. Via the lens of Hayden's relationships, (an endearing Doors-loving Jewish father, discouraging romances, close female bonds, marriage, motherhood, visits with psychics) the narrator seeks to reframe the idea of lost/found, beginnings/ ends. Eventually confronted with catastrophic grief in widowhood, she shows us the whirling perseverance of self. These works are utterly interested in intimacy with the reader, inviting us to join her for the perpetual search of love and life. *"This is my narrative, / a shelter of sentences,"* she writes in "Reframing." *"[T]o magnify the gulf between us / where the truth must lie."*

—Bianca Stone, *What is Otherwise Infinite*

Contents

LANDED

ENDANGERED

NOWHERE TO BE FOUND

OTHERWISE MISSING

SITUATED

All good dreamers pass this way some day.

— Joni Mitchell

DISLOCATED

Outlaws

I'm an unreliable narrator but I'm asking you to trust me anyway.

When I was five, the best-looking men on Ventura Boulevard could be found in photos on the walls of the post office, carwash style. I would stare up at them and wonder why all the guys I knew were clean-cut in comparison. I asked my mom which TV shows they were on.

She said, "These are mugshots, Susan. These are horse thieves, train robbers, kidnappers. That one killed his wife. What's wrong with you?"

I didn't know. To me they were scruffy and real, and I hated anything that was shiny and anyone who was polished.

Borrowing Sugar

I used to borrow sugar, or try to. Not from just anyone. From "entertainers" in the neighborhood. They lived in sprawling, ranch-style homes with aerial views, front yard aquariums and life-sized statues. Leon Russell on Woodley, The Jackson Five on Hayvenhurst, Tom Petty on Mooncrest. Affluence and intimacy, a false sense of security: That was the real Encino.

Never had a strategy, only an impulse. I wasn't even developed. Playing house with a Betsey Clark folding scene and Hallmark reusable stickers, the inspirational kind that said things like, "Every Day Is a Gift From God," "Showered with Blessings" and "I Believe in Miracles."

I was an anomaly in the West Valley, a trickster with a two-spirit nature, Technics turntable and a Barbie suitcase, jam-packed with personal belongings—a sheltered freewheeler, seeking access and the thrill of the hunt. And I was a bolter, always running away, but just for a little while.

Mostly I was a New Romantic, the sameness of my fate as yet to be determined. Love was someone else's story, carved in a spiral groove on a vinyl platter. So I borrowed sugar, or tried to. But instead, dogs barked, alarms rang out and I was escorted off Private Property, released back into "The Ranch of the Evergreens"—Los Encinos— encircled by the Transverse Ranges, surrounded by the nouveau riche.

For months, years, my measuring cup stayed empty. Roaming the streets of the 91316 where *It's a Wonderful Life* was shot. South of Ventura, Liberace had a piano shaped pool. Let me swim in it once. Called me "Sweetie." North of Valley Vista, the gulleys and ditches connecting flatland to hillside were hideouts, wishing wells of early faith:

Faith in the power of Everything, canceled out by a voice saying "You're Nothing." My brother, brazenly dealing weed and coke from his bedroom window. He tried to teach me that Goodness was impermanent, on loan. But I had love songs in my head that made Big Promises. When the lunatic moon touched my brother, converting him from a gentle boy into the Opposite of Sugar, it was songs and sweets that pulled me across.

When not borrowing, I was busy eating: Hostess cupcakes, Fruit pies, Sno Balls, Twinkies, Zingers, Donettes. I was addicted to sugar. It made me bold and shy. Empowered me. Sedated me. Borrowing sugar equaled escape from an unsafe home. Fleeing risk by risking was better than staying put.

The in-crowd lived elsewhere, that much was clear. "Over the hill" in woodsy canyons with more shade and less heat. Jackson Browne on Outpost Drive, Joni Mitchell on Appian Way. I wanted to be free and in the clouds but was exiled to Royal Oaks, with its lion's head door knockers and central air conditioning.

And I learned how to work my way in by saying, "Lend me some sugar, I am your neighbor." It was my only way around a set of circumstances—in search of the sweetness from someone else's life whose whereabouts were hidden but known to me.

That's how it started, this borrowing sugar. That's how it started, this running away.

You Make Me Feel So Young

Sam Weinstock asked for a slow dance during a family wedding at the Ventura Club in Sherman Oaks. He approached me at the dessert buffet where I was pouring chocolate syrup on a do-it-yourself hot fudge sundae.

He said he lived next door to my Aunt Goldie on Alcove Street and thought I was kind of pretty. The hired singer crooned Sinatra. As Sam twirled me, his hands on my back were like wheels of brie, smooth and effective, soft like a cow.

He was James Coburn's double. I'd seen "Ride Lonesome." I already knew my future husband would be like a steak at The Palm, a Prime Porterhouse, rough-hewn on the outside, tender underneath.

I told him I was six. He told me he was forty. I told him he smelled good. He told me he'd bought his cologne at Rexall.

I remembered Mom once saying that guys who wore Canoe by Dana were "cold and hungry."

1971 Was a Bad Year for Certain People

Into this house, we're born.
— The Doors

ONE

"Riders on the Storm" was my father's favorite Doors song
long before I'd understood its meaning.
My father was about to turn forty, had missed
the 60s altogether, that kind of music made him feel included.
He'd thought sitting in the Orchestra Pit at synagogue
would bring him closer to God, but the choir, with its *rinah u'tefillah*
—temple songs written to open the heart—pushed him away,
he was more drawn to the Fender Rhodes electric piano
pretending to be rain, my father also pretended to be rain,
dropped from Manzarek's fingertips, echo effects
from Morrison's lips into our candles on Shabbat and Hanukkah.
Year-round soundtrack, other parents were listening
to Petula Clark, Sergio Mendes & Brasil '66, Bacharach
but this Doors thing was my father's obsession, his own heart
a Venn diagram: circular, logical, somewhat closed, imposed
with decorum. And yet earthy renegades outweighed
and swayed his better judgment.

TWO

"Riders on the Storm" turned me on and terrorized
my entire childhood. Pulled me into the land of the Zodiac Killer,
HARD LUCK tattooed on the hand of Billy Cook.
Look, I wanted to love that song, but I thought it was about murder
and I was eight. Who knew this would be the coming age
of future crime sprees? Son of Sam, Ted Bundy, Hillside Strangler,
Jim Jones. Hollywood High teenaged runaway
with ligature marks, an Honors art student injected with Windex.
I already dreaded unearthly forces whose DNA and fingerprints
went undetectable in an era when Forensics meant
trying to catch someone with the limited technology of bare hands.

THREE

"Riders on the Storm" played tricks with my head
involving bloodshed and trepidation, where
I would pretend to be a victim of crime scenes, the void inside
a chalk outline. I'd seek out signs whenever in the dark,
as I practiced martial arts under the covers in a Lanz nightgown:
bending down, kicking up, punching air, a nightly bedroom prayer,
where I mastered open-hand techniques while exploring
the faceless drifter in me.

FOUR

"Riders on the Storm" blasted through a house where
everything unjust in the world was kept hidden like The War,
the horror show my father would watch on *Eyewitness News* at 6 PM.
He was oblivious of my fears and to the fact that 1971
was a bad year for certain people, including me.
He kept tuning into the song and tuning out my bleak reality,
criticized me for wearing army pants but failed to share his feelings
about combat, collateral damage, the inequity of modern men.
He guarded his kids from uglier truths of existence, would never
bring up Current Events. He'd reference The Ten Commandments,
which he knew by heart. He lionized Judaism. Had honor, courage,
strength, bestowed on us at length his personal code,
an Ethics discourse.

FIVE

"Riders on the Storm" was my father's all-time favorite Doors song,
even with Morrison's laundry list of known offenses:
indecent exposure, profanity, unpredictable scenes, mood swings,
breakdowns, asthma, ulcers, bloating, clinical despair,
with the stunted air of liquor breath and the ever-present death wish.
He'd once been a UCLA guy, like my father. Behind a desk,
folding corners of his homework into paper airplanes.
But Morrison graduated and then "dropped out."
Let's face it: The Doors embraced uncertainty.
My father was presence in reverse, immersing himself
in plans and answers. Saw an alter ego in mystical Jim,
a sliding door of what could have been had he risked
being an artist.

SIX

"Riders on the Storm" was the oft-heard song
coming from overhead speakers at my father's secret spot,
The Third Eye, a psychedelic Garden of Eden
where he'd buy me love beads.
My long waves with a middle part, yin-yang necklace,
patchwork halter top. It was a head shop selling Pop art,
Oaxacan wedding dresses, handcrafted leather.
It was Morrisonesque. Hippies and straights would commune
in the same blacklight room, drink Bonny Doon from the bottle
and stare at the posters: *Dr. Strange Meets Eternity, Lost Horizon,*
2000 Light Years From Home, Butterflies and Dogwood,
Symbology, Love is Love. Never seen colors so vibrant.
Never been high, not even close, but glow and vibrations,
ultraviolet energy made me believe I'd entered a new dimension.
There was a hand-painted school bus parked out front,
a bathtub stuffed with nasturtiums, bohemians hanging
with Vets just home from Vietnam, jamming on guitars,
reflecting on battle scars, smoking hand rolled cigarettes
and grass. I felt urgent, paid attention to their stories,
listened in, touched straggly beards. My father would say:
"Stay away from those shell-shocked men." But I didn't.

SEVEN

"Riders on the Storm" —the single—debuted on Billboard's Hot 100
in June of '71, just before that last overdub ending in Le Marais,
sending my father into situational depression.
Attached to a rock star defined by transgression, he played
the "Storm" song as a form of Kaddish. It seemed to soothe him.
The day Jim Morrison died, I sneaked out of my house
and into The Third Eye, to spy on freedom and linger
in The Bead Room, which had cracks in the cement floor
from the Sylmar earthquake. No one knew I was gone.
My eyes fixed on shelves with bowls of colored glass,
puka shells and seed beads, as I settled into a corner and listened,
not to "Riders" but to "L.A. Woman," realizing that in about ten years,
I would be one. A teenaged girl on a bean bag chair kept smiling.
I smiled back and wanted to ask, *"Are you a bohemian?"*
She could have been on the cover of *Seventeen Magazine*

with her lean frame, freckled face and empty gaze,
like Morrison's "cosmic partner," Pamela, nothing seemed
to faze her, as if she'd dropped too much of something
and was on a trip somewhere I'd never get to go.
She was a tableau of all the beautifulness one might find
on a good day in 1971, how I'd imagined a freethinker to be,
fearless and carefree, the way—not just my father—
but I dreamed of being.

EIGHT

"Riders on the Storm" began to play. The song brought
tears to the Third Eye volunteers behind the counter and the girl
was also crying. "Dying will make him more popular," she said,
twirling her hair, which was red and partially French braided.
She wore a stainless-steel bracelet with a man's name
engraved on it, saw me staring and said, "POW/MIA.
It shows a soldier's rank and date of the last time he was seen.
I mean, he's probably been blown to pieces."
Then she took the ID bracelet off her wrist, handed it over, asked me
to keep it. I sat there long after she'd left, at once bereft
at imagining the unaccounted-for army man, whose loved ones
were awaiting his arrival or death—and elated at this unlikely gift
I had been given. Later, when the bracelet was next to my skin,
alone with the lifeblood of this veteran and the absence of Jim,
I could only envision my father, who was disappeared
in a different form. I wanted more than his watchful eye, more than
having to listen to his favorite music.
I didn't know he loved me. He never said those words out loud.
Did he have to emotionally detach to shield me from harm's way? Did he
have to conform, pay the cost, by letting his own free spirit get lost
and stay Missing In Action?

Demolished

My mom took me to see "Love Story" at the Encino Theatre and in a crochet beret, I entered but didn't win the Ali MacGraw Lookalike Contest.

On the ride home she explained how wrong the advertising campaign was for that movie, that you should always (not never) say you're sorry when you love someone.

I wanted to move my bedroom furniture into the Encino Theatre and take up residence there. It was the hub of our town, with single-attraction shows and a thousand seats.

By the mid-70s it was mowed down to build a high-rise office building. My Encino was gone. It became a business district, like what was happening all over Los Angeles, like so much of America.

Welcome Wagon

Covered in garbage, I crawled out of the trash can and pretended nothing had happened. There were other kids around but nobody said anything, nobody even laughed.

I'd been scrubbed, tossed in and called a "Jew-girl" by Julie Medina. She'd grabbed me from behind, tore my clothes, lifted me up and threw me in.

It was the end of the first day of 7th grade at Mulholland Junior High in Van Nuys.

When I got home, I couldn't get out of bed for three days.
"I'm never going back," I told my parents.

But there was no further discussion. They didn't think to transfer me to the safer school in our neighborhood. There was no meeting with a counselor or therapist to address the state I was in. My father didn't believe in therapy.

My mom finally said, "When I was your age, a girl punched me in the face and gave me a fat lip. I was humiliated but forced myself to show up the next day and stay strong. You need to do the same. Fuck her! Don't give her any power. Pull yourself together. You can do it!"

So I did.

For the Love of Captain Trips

He's gone, gone, nothing's gonna bring him back. He's gone.
— Robert Hunter/Jerome Garcia

I knew this kid who could play guitar
and sing like God,
only he thought Jerry Garcia was God.

Holding his middle finger down
against the center of his palm,
sticking the other fingers up
like the flipping-off sign,
the fuck you sign, only backwards.

Trying to be like Garcia,
who lost half his middle finger
in a wood chopping accident
when he was four.

Garcia's Disciple was a true believer.
Sitting in a puddle of Summer-camp-sweat,
see-sawing to the imaginary Dead beat
that played in his head.
I believed that we were living proof
of time travel.

We were *The Last Waltz*
(Part Two).

I was a Jewish Joni Mitchell,
an underage lady of Malibu canyon,
weeds that passed for flowers
wrapped like a wreath
around shoulder-length hair.
Drinking "A Case of You,"
I mean him.

He wore a tie-dye t-shirt
with an abstract skeleton
leaning against a San Francisco bus stop.
It read: Don't HAIGHT me because I'm beautiful.
He wore an Uncle Sam top hat
pinned with a mini-American flag
in the spirit of "Captain Trips."

He was the half-brother of Mickey Hart,
a Rhythm Devil
and one of the Dead's drummers.
That gave him credibility.
That made him *mishpokhe*.

He spoke like he had laryngitis.
His hair looked like SpaghettiOs.
His eyes were multi-flecked, Fourth of July
sparklers that burned right back
at me while changing colors.

I told him: Communication was liner notes
on printed envelopes that contained my records.
Cat Stevens, my intended.
Carly Simon, a surrogate mother.
Gordon Lightfoot, sage of the community.
The Carpenters, my second family.

He opened his wallet, showed me a picture
with his arm around Garcia.
God wasn't supposed to have a missing finger
and tour internationally.

This was Camp J.C.A., Malibu
where we all wore white on Friday night,
lit candles for Shabbat.
Where we were taught that God is one
and one is God.

I didn't go to Hebrew school for eight years
to finally see God in a photo booth snapshot,
dazed and confused, a huge pot belly,
mutton chop whiskered sideburns
and a psychedelic smile,
smoking a doobie with his compadres—
or did I?

And yeah, I'd heard that song "Truckin'"
played endlessly
on my own brother's Tijuana ukulele.
I knew who the Grateful Dead were
and they meant nothing to me.

But that night, Garcia's Disciple
took out a left-handed Gibson
with worn out backstage passes on it
from every World Tour since 1969
and played, "Box of Rain" by campfire
(in between "You've Got a Friend,"
"Leaving on a Jet Plane" and "Circle Game").

We all joined hands, formed a prayer circle.
He led the service in song
and everyone was bonded
by the scripture
of acoustic communion.

After, he walked me back to G-7
the all-girl bunkhouse
and on the way, I got my moon
for the very first time, drops trickling down
in a long, thin stream. "Drops of the body
and the blood of what is holy," he said,
an unlikely statement from a Kosher Jew.

It was a short period,
one of embarrassment.
I'd become an official woman:
ripped open at the core, humiliated,
exposed.

That winter, Garcia's Disciple took me
to a Dead show at The Shrine Auditorium.
I got to ride in the back of his friend's pick-up
and smoke my first clove cigarette.

I went backstage
to meet Bob Weir and God.
God was quiet, walked right past me,
closed the door, but through the crack
that he'd left open, I watched
as he stood, needle in hand.

I got my first contact high.
It lasted twenty years.

Have you ever seen a full-grown man
give up his soul and life force
to the music?
Make you believe that there is a God
or at least a messenger?

Garcia is dead tonight,
an ungrateful end to a jam-packed life.
Designing ties, breaking ties
but always the connective
tissue, the hook and the eye.

Passenger Was the Encore

(Shrine Auditorium/January 11, 1978)

It's just like Woodstock here: six thousand Deadheads and no hate, no judgment. In this psychedelic church, everyone is smiling.

"Bertha" plays for thirty-five minutes. The shoulder of Garcia's Disciple keeps brushing up against mine. Is this my first date?

I pray for him to put down the air guitar and kiss me. He never does.

Her Will

was written with a BIC Banana on personalized stationery when we were ten. She planned to kill herself. None of it seemed real. It was like stepping out of time.

It all started when her dad said he "wanted a fresh start with new surroundings." He spoke like he was reading from a real estate brochure. He'd recently joined the Ferrari Club of America. Left their house on Addison Street and headed north on the 101 in his Dino 246 GT to his new family in Calabasas, a concrete village he had developed from dirt roads and shacks, filled it with Mediterranean-style subdivisions, stolen its core. He was an international architect, created whole neighborhoods. Won the Golden Nugget Award. The Home of the Year Award. But he never built a space and stayed long enough to make *her* feel safe.

She was leaving her mom a hopeful watercolor she'd painted, called "Kimmi's Clouds." It showed how she imagined the sky, without pollution. She was leaving her brother the key to her "Have A Nice Day" smiley face diary. She was leaving me the trendy clothes her dad had bought her on their love-replacement shopping sprees: Chemin de Fers from Fred Segal. Silk blouses from Maxfield Bleu. Her Laura Ashley everything. They wouldn't have fit. She was four sizes smaller.

When she handed me the other half of our 14-karat gold Mizpah charm, the one we'd split the year before, I thought *I* would die. It was a lopsided heart with a jagged edge. We wore it on gold chains around our necks to show the other kids at school that we were part of a two-piece set. In Hebrew, *mizpah* means watchtower. It also means emotional bond. I could not imagine the world without her. It was she I counted on most. I was that person for her too. So, I wouldn't open my hand to take the charm. That would have meant accepting her decision. That would have made me her accomplice.

I needed to talk to an adult. But her mom wasn't home. I had to change her mind, prove that there were reasons she mattered. I begged her to tell me what she valued: about herself, about her life. She couldn't think of anything. I made a list in my head of all that I loved about her, the longest list I'd ever made about anything. There was so much to love. Little things. Big things. Unseeable things. I spoke that list to her, named everything I could think of.

She listened. Even laughed a little. Then, I made a cave with my arms, cocooned her. Her body shook at first and soon it softened. She put the pen down. We stayed like that, in silence, for what felt like hours.

***

In thirty years to come, her dad would get a secret facelift. He'd tell his daughter that he was going in for a minor procedure. He'd have a stroke on the operating table, get Locked-in syndrome. The doctor finished the surgery anyway.

She would ask me to accompany her to the hospital, thinking it would cheer him up. Her dad's face looked a perfect thirty-five. His whole body, paralyzed. But his brain: still working. I could see he recognized me, though it had been years. I would talk to him about beloved Southern California architects: Colcord, Lautner, Gesner. How on every birthday, I would seek out and drive to a home of architectural note from an old movie or TV show and it would remind me of him.

His eyes would light up. He couldn't speak but he could see and hear and understand. His new, flawless face showed signs of sorrow and regret. It was like at last he had the right words for his daughter, yet he couldn't speak them. This would be the end of her.

The Jeane Dixon Effect

*The year The Doobie Brothers released "*What a Fool Believes*" was the same year my mom and all her friends got into psychics. They believed in supernatural people who could lead you back to yourself. There was Malka Lipshutz, the cashier at Fromin's Deli who moonlighted as a handwriting analyst for the LAPD. There was Dolores Cardelucci, a clairvoyant who practiced psychometry and had a who's who of celebrity clients who hung on her every word.*

Mom would invite me with her on these outings.

Dolores would take our watches, rings and bracelets into her bathroom, close the door and sit with them there while we waited for answers in her sunny kitchen. Then she'd return and analyze the energy that emanated from our jewelry. She was never not accurate.

Mom taught me that "faith in things unseen" wasn't a concept that just applied to religion. She encouraged me to trust my intuition, that we all had ESP and it was there for us to use if only we chose to listen to ourselves.

You should try it sometime.

UNAVAILABLE

Leveling Up

I was never a trailblazer in the 70s, though I sure tried hard to look like one. I was not confident enough to loiter at Westworld Arcade. I'd tip-toe around it, peek in a little, lean against the open doorway, then freeze in position. You'd think I was trying to sneak into the Pussycat Theater.

I knew that everything I "wasn't" was waiting for me inside if I dared enter: Asteroids, Super Breakout, Night Driver, Canyon Bomber, Pursuit, Tail Gunner, Head On, Crash 'N Score, Gotcha, Qwak!

Forty years later, I still get shy walking into new rooms.

The Soul Section

You can't sing about love unless you know about it.
— Billy Eckstine

It was easy to believe that everyone in the world was Jewish.

That's how I felt growing up in Encino and my parents planned for it that way. We had The Deli, shuls with pools and high school girls sporting the exact same nose job.

There was a clear code to follow that I couldn't interpret in a way that served me. I wanted more of something but I wasn't sure what. So even in the requisite designer clothes I stood out, grasping for the intangible.

My family was considered upper-middle class, fringe society. We went out to dinner each Sunday night without fail, to Ah Fong's, Love's Barbeque, Barone's or El Torito. We had everything delivered: prescriptions, dry cleaning, Adohr Farms milk, platters of cold cuts.

Dad was an entertainment attorney, his style, hipster Rabbi in cowboy boots. Strict and opinionated, generous to a fault, he made enough money to drive a two-seater Mercedes and wear a signature Rolex. He'd take us to Hawaii every summer and let me charge on his Neiman Marcus card.

He was also the proud owner of a weekend toupee.

I couldn't bring boys home because they'd always fall for Mom.

She was graceful and vivacious, a skinny fit model. She'd say, "I'm not into the heavy eating scene like your father and the rest of his family." She didn't teach me how to cook or to sew, but she was a teacher of "poise" at the Dorothy Shreve School of Modeling and Charm in Sherman Oaks.

Her days unfolded with an effortlessness that was not passed on to me.

I was a boy-crazy girl with a series of crushes on unavailable older men, like waiters, hairdressers, soap opera stars. There was simply no one at Birmingham High. Love wasn't to be found anywhere west of Sepulveda. It was waiting in Westwood Village, or so I'd heard.

I wasn't a fox but I wasn't a dog.

Personality-wise, I was offbeat with an edge. When I finally got the courage to make the big trek to The City, I'd just turned sixteen. I believed free expression took place away from my neighborhood. I looked forward to getting to be "me" somewhere else, and if that didn't work, to reinvention.

For most of my friends, the upgrade from a love life in The Flats was landing a boy from Beverly Hills, a doctor's son, whose parents were members of Hillcrest Country Club and Temple Israel.

For me, love's blueprint came from records I played on a turntable from Fedco. Acoustic music of my generation presented a newfound, sensitive male. Cat Stevens, James Taylor, Jackson Browne and Dan Fogelberg were unafraid to expose their feelings.

I was seeking someone who knew nothing about the unwanted geek I was. I wouldn't admit I lived north of Sunset, north of Mulholland, north of Valley Vista. I'd pretend I was from Malibu.

But my guy wouldn't care. He'd be able to see past my geography and concave chest, my soft, unwanted curves—right through to my soul.

I invited Pepper Goldberg to explore with me. She was an on-again/off-again friend, a hothouse flower with swinging, divorced parents and temperamental tendencies. I'd spend time with her on nights when Kimmi had other plans.

Nobody offered to drive us to Westwood, so we had to take the RTD. That meant an hour and half on the 405, where I couldn't escape Mom's voice in my head, like the soundtrack of *A Chorus Line*, instructing me on how to attract the opposite sex.

My mom got everything she wanted (even when she didn't want it) and seemed content the majority of the time. She was a romantic of the highest order with rules to live by, culled from her teachings at the modeling school, Yiddish humor, and her own bare-bones experience as a *Cosmo*-lovin' woman:

1) Upon entering a room, don't look from side to side. Never make eye contact. Walk with your head held high.

2) Look for boys of your same race and religion. Love is complicated enough. Begin with a common denominator.

3) If you want your dreams to come true, don't sleep.

The lowdown on The Village was widely known: the hippest kids were inside the Arcade or at Wherehouse Records. Vals were at Stan's Donuts or tucked away in a booth at Hamburger Hamlet. A mix of artistic stoners and Gucci Girls flocked to Postermat.

A glass case with a selection of paraphernalia greeted the customers. Vintage and brand-new posters of rock stars, movies and concerts were all up for grabs, as well as buttons with catch phrases from current and bygone eras. And Postermat had the best-looking guys I'd ever seen.

They'd lean against walls, some flirting, others debating the economic downturn of the energy crisis.

It was packed like a concert at the Fabulous Forum. The song "Baby, I Love Your Way" by Peter Frampton was playing full blast. I walked in, looking ahead instead of around, but got distracted and broke Mom's Number One rule by having extended eye contact with an employee.

His energy was frisky, the way he'd pull a hand-blown hash pipe out from behind the counter and bounce over to a potential customer, then slink back to the cash register like he was doing The Hustle.

"What are you looking for?" he asked.

"I have no idea. I do love music. Music…is my boyfriend."

"You'd like my dad. He's an acclaimed jazz singer. I play drums, classical percussion, keyboards, bass guitar…and I sing."

"Wow. I don't play anything. Except records."

"Ever heard of Roberta Flack and Donny Hathaway?"

"Oh my God. 'Where Is The Love' is the best song ever."

"Hey, I got a great poster of the two of them. Wanna see it?"

"I'd love to."

"Meet me in the Soul Section," he said, then winked and walked away.

I glanced at Pepper, who'd been rolling her eyes and glaring.

"Who do you think you are, Andrea Silver?" she sniped.

She was referring to this nonconformist I quietly admired from Taft High, who supposedly had a one-nighter with Jermaine Jackson at the Heritage Hotel in Sherman Oaks. She'd told one friend about him in graphic detail and within seconds, the word spread all the way to Birmingham High. While I longed for her daring, who cared what kind of boxers Jermaine wore? J.J. (as he was known) lived two blocks from me with his siblings and their parents. Fans would park outside their house and wait for them to pull in or pull out.

Don't think I wasn't aware that I'd ignored Mom's Number Two rule. I'd found a City Guy who didn't treat me like a Val, who was drawn to part of me, or the real me. He just happened to be a different color.

"This is where I want to live. Right here," he told me, referring to the specific aisle where Marvin Gaye and Aretha Franklin shared a shelf with Bessie Smith and Billie Holiday.

I'd heard of these singers from my dad, who had a collection of 33s, 45s and 78s he used to play at night when he'd get home from work. It was a way for him to relax, until he found Transcendental Meditation and started listening to eight track tapes of gongs and rhythms of the rainforest.

In the Soul Section, we sat on the floor and huddled close, his arm half around me as he spoke.

"Dad played with Dizzy Gillespie and Dexter Gordon, Miles Davis and Charlie Parker. He'd lived many lives before moving to the Valley."

"Wait. I live there! I thought you were a city guy."

"I am now, but I grew up in Encino. We were the first black family there, before the Jacksons moved in. I'm a 'JBA'—Jew By Association."

I couldn't believe I hadn't seen him in the produce department at Gelson's or browsing the bins of Sunshine Records.

He possessed an open-air kindness that was fresh and new to me. His spirit was fragrant as the Dreams oil they sold in small bottles right around the corner.

"I've known a lot of Jewish girls. You sure are a beautiful one," he said, taking my hand.

"Me?"

"You," he said.

Pepper was waiting outside, with a scowl instead of a smile. As I walked toward her, an arm reached out and handed me the Flack/ Hathaway poster and a piece of paper with a phone number on it.

"Call me tomorrow before you go out for brunch, because I know that's what you do in Encino on a Sunday."

Pepper's dad, Jerry Goldberg, was our ride home. He pulled up in his mid-life-crisis Datsun 280Z, squished us both into the passenger seat and surprised us with tickets to see a late night show of *Pat Collins – The Hip Hypnotist* at the Celebrity Club on Sunset. I forgot to call my parents to say I wouldn't be back until after my midnight curfew.

At 2 AM, as I tiptoed inside the house, Mom and Dad were robed shadows against the French windows, searching for signs of City trouble.

"Where the hell have you been?" Dad asked, stern but not yelling.

"I'm sorry. We went to see this wacky hypnotist and she put me in a trance and my mind went blank."

"Pat Collins? I hear she's the real thing!" Mom said. "Evelyn and Sy Berenbaum went to that show. Sy got onstage and confessed to an affair he'd had ten years ago with his personal secretary."

"You should have called beforehand to get my permission," Dad said. "Divorcées have different rules than I do."

"I won't do it again. Oh, we also went to Postermat where I met and fell hard for someone named Guy Eckstine. His dad is an acclaimed jazz singer."

"Billy Eckstine? Mr B.? Was he ever handsome," Mom said.

"So is his son."

"He's…" My dad paused, choosing his words carefully. "…from a different world. You can't go out with him. You can't go out with *anyone* who isn't Jewish."

I ran to my room, taped my new poster to the wall, climbed into bed and turned on my Flack/Hathaway album. I cried about otherness and two tribes, about racial divide. I cried about railcars and cattle cars, about being chained and being branded.

We weren't so different, were we?

I wanted to call Guy to tell him I'd be at Postermat next Saturday night and I'd meet him in the Soul Section, where we both wanted to live.

But I didn't. I went to sleep, breaking Mom's third and final rule, the one about having to stay awake to dream.

The next morning, all I could think of, besides Guy Eckstine, was the power my father had over me that I wasn't able to reconcile. You didn't want to make him angry. Monotone speech would be reinforced by a death stare.

If I wasn't allowed to go out with Guy Eckstine, I could create a home movie in my head where we're meeting at Alice's Restaurant in Westwood, reading lyrics back and forth from "The Closer I Get to You." I'm wearing a padded Teenform bra, certain that greater depths of closeness await.

Soon, we're shacking up at the Encino Travelodge and he's looking into my eyes with intention, saying lines I'd only heard characters use on *All My Children*. I notice that his boxers have mini-Stratocasters on them. We're making plans for me to move out of my parents' house and into his apartment when Dad shows up in his 450 SL and drags me to the hidden chambers of our Temple.

It is there I receive a talk from our rabbi about not going outside of one's race to look for love. It's the final scene, where the audience realizes these two outsiders from separate ethnic groups have taken a chance on each other only to find themselves once again persecuted.

It was in Dad's stack of albums under Elvis and the Mills Brothers that I uncovered none other than Billy Eckstine! On the record's sleeve, there was a picture of him, handsome as ever, and a quote underneath it that read, *The First Romantic Black Male Sings His Heart Out.*

That night, I invited Dad into my room and played Mr. B. on my turntable. We both sat listening as a haunting voice, low and velvety smooth, sang to us about being a "Prisoner of Love."

And I watched as the tension left Dad's face, as his cheeks flushed with interest, as a closed mind opened ever so slightly.

"Eckstine was the real thing. When he was living in Chicago and I was a kid, I got to see him perform with Earl Hines at The Grand Terrace Café. The place was run by Capone. It was called a black and tan club. It wasn't segregated. You could co-mingle there."

"What a concept."

"I love this song. And how you make me think…"

Then the record ended.

I waited until the lights were off in my parents' bedroom to make the call. I knew that when Guy Eckstine heard my voice, he'd ask me out and I would say YES. And I would go. It didn't matter to me anymore how my father felt about it.

Hit'lahavut or How to Say Ardor in Hebrew

A worn thread linked me to my religious upbringing: Temple, a "She who wears the best dress to High Holidays wins" kind of a place with services entirely in Hebrew, same length as a Grateful Dead concert.

Sunday School was where I went to meet and make out with dark, secretive boys, smoke clove cigarettes in the Ladies' Room during Torah study and gossip with other full-bodied, restless girls.

At Valley Beth Shalom, I struggled to accept that I was one of the chosen people as it didn't seem fair to the people who weren't chosen. So, I searched for a light I could count on, and somehow found it, in the astonishing glimmers that came from the sanctuary's stained glass windows, incandescent depictions conveying mysteries of the Sh'ma—without words.

The Future of Porn Chic

I really had to act, 'cause I didn't have any lines.
— Marilyn Chambers

The day I met the era's most popular adult film star, I stole my Grandma Rosey's Lady Schick, the gold-tinted one with the gentle action shaving head and proceeded to decimate my bush. This was 10th grade, I was fifteen. This was when girls and women still had bushes.

That same year, I'd spent an entire weekend away from the West Valley, camped out in the flats of Beverly Hills at a porn producer's apartment. My friend Fritzy's Uncle Sid was notorious for hardcore and sexploitation. He was going out of town on a movie shoot and had a Saint Bernard named Larceny that needed to be fed. He'd offered Fritzy a C-note if she could "watch over things."

We didn't even have our learner's permits yet. We had to bum a ride from Royal Oaks to Plastic Surgery Row, where Sid lived. Once we got there, I felt trapped. We only knew the abbreviated stretch of road we'd take by bus, back and forth from Studio City to Woodland Hills.

But the RTD that ran along Olympic, Santa Monica Boulevard and Wilshire was flat-out intimidating to navigate. I wanted to go shopping at Bonwit Teller, eat chopped salads at La Scala Boutique, get my hair done by Gene Shacove.

"No, Gidget." Fritzy said. That was her nickname for me, the Little Girl with Big Ideas. In truth, she was the one who hatched all the plans and I should have known, she already had one: taking taxis to and from Nibbler's for breakfast, lunch and dinner, and binge-watching Uncle Sid's private collection on his Sony Betamax. He had a treasure-trove that could stun a serial killer, smut that everyone else, in those days, had to go to the Valley Adult Theatre in their trench coats to view. This was before the rise of home video. This was the Golden Age of Porn.

I'd been raised in a high-end *shtetl* but had met more than my share of garden variety perverts just walking into Encino Bowl in broad daylight on any given day. I'd seen a lot for my age, plenty, but that weekend learned fast that I knew nothing.

It was a non-stop peep show of bushy women and swarthy men—*The Devil in Miss Jones, The Opening of Misty Beethoven, Inside Jennifer Welles, The Private Afternoons of Pamela Mann*—where we discovered every idea not included in the book *Everything You Always Wanted to Know About Sex* (*But Were Afraid to Ask*), every kind of person we could share our bodies with—and everything, real or synthetic, we could insert inside of ourselves or someone else. This was all news to us.

Our main obsession during those forty-eight hours on Lasky Drive was the naked leading lady we were struck by. Just "your basic girl next door" as she'd call herself at some point, in an interview. But before becoming a legend in the porn industry, Marilyn Chambers was The Ivory Soap Girl, the "99 & 44/100% pure girl."

And she was only ten years older than us.

Fritzy had classified info about a Chambers movie-in-the-works that only insiders were aware of, rumored to be the matchless barrier-breaker. It hadn't been written yet. It wouldn't ever be written. It would be played out, in sex scenes, one after the other after the other after the other.

It was to be directed by Monty Mitchell, also known as Uncle Sid!

Back to my bush. Or lack thereof.

Shaving was a mystery to me. I'd strip and spread out in front of the mirrored closet doors of my ten-by-ten cell—my bedroom—and wonder, when the time came, would the love of my life look that closely at me or were the lights always out during sex? How much did presentation matter?

My question was soon answered, indirectly, by Uncle Sid of all people.

See, Fritzy had failed to mention that when he was in town, he'd use her family's backyard in Encino for still shots and for filming.

Nothing could have prepared me for what happened a couple of months after our erotic immersion in Beverly Hills, the day Fritzy would invite me over for what seemed like a typical afterschool experience: make snacks, make prank phone calls, drink Tab and read *Playgirl*.

Fritzy lived on Adlon Drive, in a mid-century modern on a corner lot with an almond shaped pool and wraparound view. That afternoon, when I walked into her house rambling on about the yentas at Everywoman's Village who'd kicked me out of Jazzercise for not keeping time, she interrupted by saying, "Whatever you do, don't go outside. They're filming a trailer for the new movie. We're underage. We could get arrested for being here."

I kind of wanted to be handcuffed. I kind of wished I was the one starring in that film. I knew it was trashy, beneath me, "for lowlifes," as my mom would say. But I longed to cross over into something where I too was undressed and it was unpredictable, something the complete opposite of that cage that confined me, the one I'd been trying to break free from since 4th grade: Encino.

"I have a surprise for you," Fritzy said, taking my hand, leading me to her bathroom. She pointed to a mound of what looked like two inches of dirty blonde cat hair that had gathered on the linoleum floor.

"These are Marilyn Chambers' pubes. Johnny 'the Wadd' Holmes is here, and he told her 'Times have changed' and he 'couldn't get it up for a bush anymore.' So she shaved it all off. Now she looks ten. Uncle Sid approves. He said, 'Without all that hair there you can see everything. Our audience is ready for that.' "

"I want to meet her," I blurted out. "She's had a rough go of it. We could help pull her into the mainstream."

"They're busy in the backyard. Johnny's got Marilyn bent over the diving board and he's coming in from behind. Bet you didn't know that sodomy is illegal in certain states."

"Can we watch from your bedroom window?" I asked.

"No, Gidget. Uncle Sid said he'd pay me to clean up her mess."

"I think if we gather this pile into some Saran Wrap, we could list it in the Recycler and make a killing," I told Fritzy, proud of initiating an idea.

Fritzy got down on her hands and knees, scooped it all up like an obedient housewife with an edge. "We get to make our own choices now," she said, waving the baggie in my face. "It's all about shaved bush. I'm buying a razor and reshaping history!"

45

Expert (Yes, You)

Ricky Birnbaum taught me that the proper way to apply eyeliner was also the proper way to get a man to fall in love with you. He said: "Tilt your head back slightly and bring your eyes to a half-open state."

I Wanted Him

I hate to think I been blinded baby
Why can't I see you tonight?
— Jimmy Page/John Paul Jones/Robert Plant

I wanted him:
this guy who sliced meat into cold cuts
at Encino Deli—
bologna, salami, pastrami, belly lox
no socks, no underwear
crisp white t-shirt without stains
careless and low slung 501s
careless, before it was Kool

I wanted him:
this cross between William Katt
in *Carrie*
and a Dickensian parish boy
I'd been sneaking looks at *The Joy of Sex*
in my parents' hidden cabinet
and he became the person
I'd picture it with

I wanted him:
he was larger than life
Surround sound
looked like he'd been around
and around
Peter Frampton, Roger Daltrey, Robert Plant
every golden-haired rock icon
rolled into one
and even behind that counter
he was Someone

I wanted him:
through the chocolate phosphates
the bialy specials, the Halvah bars
—and was pulled in
by the way he'd stare at me

He'd stare at me through my entire meal
and it made me feel
Seen

I wanted him:
for I was used to Mama's Boys
the price of their toys
their bragging rights
their allowances
their five and ten year plans
Where were the cowboys
on my brother's flannel pajamas?
Where were the lumberjacks
from *Here Come the Brides*?

I wanted him:
there was no hiding it
My mom had taught me
to fall in love with love
not where to find it
not how to work it
LOVE as the only answer
Her bible was a book of poems called
There are Men Too Gentle to Live Among Wolves

I wanted him:
because when I would try and imagine
the men in those poems
the ones my mom seemed to long for
I wondered
What was wrong with them?
Why weren't they stoned
and reckless?
Those were the kind that I leaned towards

I wanted him:
as he'd stand on his feet
for hours at a time
while the neighborhood zhlubs
whined
that the Nova was "too salty"
I knew he was deep beneath the drugs
durable, too
and the only other non-Jew I knew
besides my best friend
yet the more caring I was, the less
he stared

I wanted him:
to press me up against
the old Encino oak
but when I spoke, it was clear
I was a virgin on the pill
still waiting for the right
first
My bible was a book of poems
called *My Song for Him
Who Never Sang to Me*
The men in those poems
weren't gentle or reckless
just hit-n-run absentees

I wanted him:
to deliver bags of bialys
to my house
comp my egg creams
drink Club Margaritas from
the same can
He was the only man who could
pull the Tel Aviv out of me
straighten my curls
make me Norwegian
like he was

I wanted him:
to give me a ride in his VW bug
that during a flash flood
rolled down Laurel Canyon
by itself
crashed into a series of parked cars
and survived
Even with his hands in the pepper-beef
turkey breast, lean strips of tongue
it was 1979, I was sixteen years
young
Had a brother who beat me
with words and his fists
and I saw this post-modern
Oliver Twist
as my way out of
the Valley

I wanted him:
to undress me in his car
and teach me the secret
to dreaming
so I stole all my dad's quarters
cashed them in for dollar bills
took the RTD to
the Whole Earth Marketplace
and bought him a glass bong
then I read *The Sensuous Woman*
(memorized the tricks)
and asked him
to please take me to the Styx concert

I wanted him:
so I didn't tell my folks
that after the show
we would go back to his apartment
in Tarzana
where I would bring not only
my mood ring
but my new revered record
In Through the Out Door

by Led Zep
It was common knowledge
that if you took a wet rag
and rubbed it against the album's
inner sleeve
it would leave behind
the black and white drawings
transform them to
permanently colored

I wanted him:
as if being in his presence
seemed to heal me
from convention, certainty
and excess
It was nothing less than awakening
to muffled speech that
revealed itself in reverse
backmasking and lock grooves
were all the rage and I was
underage
decoding subliminal messages
from album covers,
imagining older men as lovers,
navigating firsts

I wanted him:
even as it hurt in his bed
I focused on what I could see
His hair, golden movie star
ringlets
that smelled like Flex shampoo
his hands too
away from the meat cutting machine
far more serene than one would think
his body, sinewy and covered
in freckles
"Kisses from God," Mom called them
I had 'em too

I wanted him:
though his girlfriend stared
at us
from her senior portrait
so he turned it around
made her face the wall
As I recall, when it was over
I wasn't invited back for a year
What's become clear is that for
half my life
I carried him along as blueprint
and in those I've loved
there has always been a hint
of the grown-up orphan
the waiflike fable boy groomed
on the street
Who knew his touch would
unseat me?

I wanted him:
still, so I'd try things out on
other men
some who signed their lives away
on me
let me steal their wild for free
The Butterfly Flick
The Show-Don't-Tell
Afraid of the slow-down,
the love scene
I'd try things out on other men
and think, One day I'll
come back
and show you
what I've learned
I didn't care that he wanted
nothing
to do with me

I wanted him:
all because
when he'd stare at me
from behind that counter
I felt seen.

Instead of Observing the Sabbath

my father would drive me to Neiman Marcus in Beverly Hills
where on Saturdays, they offered free samples in their gourmet food section.
We gorged on caramel corn and rumaki.
He'd peel the bacon off.
We bonded over food.
We argued about religion.

He'd say, "Eating is a sacred act."
He'd add, "God will start to matter as you get older and lose people."
He'd ask, "Are you going to finish that?"
He was Santa Claus crossed with Nachman of Breslov.
All my girlfriends had crushes on him.

Stuffed

I wasn't into drugs and alcohol like everyone else. I was raised in a milk-without-meat kosher household, restricted, so I'd sidestep. I ate my way through the Valley: chocolate sodas, greasy cheeseburgers and salty fries at Fire Brigade. The Zoo and Pig's Trough at Farrell's, whether it was someone's birthday or not.

And Mike's Pizza. I'd stare through the window, watch the chef in action and pretend I was the dough that he was tossing, twirling, kneading instead of what I felt like, the sawdust beneath his feet.

I ate to fill a blank, one I felt in the form of a gaping hole I couldn't name.

The Beautiful Ugly
for Ruthie and for Kimmi

"Love yourself, move your body and watch your portions," he instructed.

Richard Simmons was only a local celebrity in 1978, just months before he would explode onto the scene and become internationally known, and stay in the limelight for forty years, until he couldn't hang on to himself anymore.

We were ten leotarded 11th graders, dancing to the beat of "Macho Man" during a private class in his exercise studio. It was the Sweet Sixteen of my oldest friend, Ruthie. Her calligraphy invitation read: *Come join me in Beverly Hills for a workout at Anatomy Asylum and for salads at Ruffage.*

This was a complete departure from the usual lavish luncheons for such an occasion, wealth displays that defined the bourgeoisie of the West Valley.

Ruthie and I lived around the corner from each other since six months old. We were thrown together by our mothers out of convenience. We weren't anything alike, which made us more like sisters. Our alliance was cemented at age five, when we nearly drowned together in my family pool. No one was watching as we traveled from the shallow end to the deep end and sunk. Her father, a non-swimmer, looked up and realized he couldn't see us. He jumped in and saved our lives!

She was (and still is) my most well adjusted friend. In high school, she got an "A" in Health, was a member of World for Women fitness center and ate half a grapefruit a day. She knew, early on, how to take care of herself, from the inside out.

She remains my compass and my anchor.

The ideal beauty of the era was slender and tan with big boobs and long, flowing hair, preferably blonde. I was a Synagogue girl; pale, flat and chubby. I hated exercising. I did own a wardrobe of Danskins that I wore as "regular clothing." *Danskins are not just for dancing.* I favored their wrap-around skirt, had one in every color.

In 1970, the average age a girl started dieting was fourteen. I was the Queen of the Crash: Scarsdale, Atkins, Stillman, The Cookie Diet, The Cabbage Soup Diet, The Sexy Pineapple Diet, The Beverly Hills Diet, The Israeli Army Diet, AYDS appetite suppressant candy. And Dexatrim.

55

I used my body sparingly, in gym class at Birmingham High when I wasn't busy faking an injury, and the night I got naked and underneath a twenty-year-old man, losing my virginity in the name of true love, only to find out it was a one-off.

By fifteen, I'd been touched *without* my consent three times: first, by a babysitter when I was eight; at twelve, at a slumber party by someone thirty-six, who fingered me in the dark while I was sleeping; and at fourteen, when a friend's older brother violently pounced on me, covering my mouth, holding me down, calling me a slut, groping and threatening me. I successfully fought him off but he left deep, bloody scratches I covered up with Joe Blasco's TVC 15 Neutralizer.

I managed to hang on to myself.

These secrets were stuffed away in emotional drawers. There were no confessional talk shows on TV and recovered memories weren't in style yet. Mom listened to Dr. Toni Grant on KABC constantly, and though I was tempted to phone in my laundry list and ask her for help, she seemed anti-feminist to me.

It was different than it is now. Kids weren't given clear-cut skills to use in the event of a transgression. People got away with all kinds of things without ever getting caught.

My body felt like a vandalized temple. I learned to wear weight as a shield, was a master of camouflage.

"Thanksgiving is this Thursday," Richard Simmons warned us. "You know what that means: everyone gains five pounds. You know you're going to overeat. You must try extra hard today. That means YOU," he shouted, pointing at *me*, even though I was positioned in the back of the room, hoping to disappear into the wallpaper like a Francesca Woodman self-portrait.

I was mortified at being seen in tights and a leotard in front of my friends.

Sprawled out next to me was Kimmi, a natural at warm-ups, stretches and dance routines. Her Mom had been teaching calisthenics in their living room, with no mirrors, since her parents' divorce.

Kimmi was my bright angel. We became inseparable in 4th grade, when I lured her into collaborating with me on a "publication" I was creating. It was a mixture of my dad's two mainstay magazines, *Playboy* and *Sports Illustrated*. I called it *Sex Illustrated* and together, we'd draw unclothed stick figures with exaggerated body parts in compromising positions.

Once we'd found each other, me and Kimmi, we would never let go. She was a combination platter of Farrah, Brigitte and Olivia Newton-John. She lived on Figurines, those crunchy diet bars. She was seventy-five pounds and swore by Nice'n Easy, with impossible blue eyes, narrow hips and enormous tits, real ones.

But she never felt like she was enough.

The girls at school thought she was conceited and kept their distance. They didn't realize she was shy and insecure. It was hard for anyone to grasp that someone who looked like she did could be plagued with self doubt. I didn't fit in anywhere either, and she gave me a place to fill. It was her breathlessness, her open heart and her willingness to connect that drew me to her. There was nothing like belonging.

Richard Simmons, in his black tank unitard, was sizing up Kimmi like she was the only girl in the room. After class, we gathered at the Ruffage salad bar, but Richard Simmons grabbed Kimmi and dragged her away from the party to a woman with frosted hair and a fake looking face who'd been waiting to meet her. She wasn't wearing a Danskin. The three of them huddled together for fifteen minutes.

I was about to get in line for "seconds" when Kimmi returned, blushing and frazzled.

"I was just invited to pose for *Playboy*," she blurted out. "That *lady* I've been talking with is their photo editor. She's on the Great Playmate Hunt, scouting nationwide for a centerfold for their 25th anniversary issue. She thinks I'm IT. Playmate of the Year! I don't know what she sees in me."

Ruthie's mom announced that it was time to open presents. She'd brought a Hansen's birthday cake but everyone was too embarrassed to eat it in front of Richard Simmons, so she decided to leave it in the car. Someone gave Ruthie an oversized satin pillow in the shape of a Baby Ruth candy bar. It got tossed around Ruffage like a volleyball and within minutes, was in shreds.

"So. Are you gonna spread your legs for *Playboy*?" I asked Kimmi.

"It's tempting,' she said. "She offered me *thousands* of dollars. I told her, 'I'm only sixteen.' She said they'd work around it, I could lie about my age. I told her *my dad* reads that magazine. I don't want him to open the centerfold, start beating off and realize it's me. I said NO. Even for that much money."

I was proud of Kimmi and stunned by her flash decision. She'd wanted to be celebrated for something since grade school. This could have been her big break, her ticket to becoming a Bond girl or a game show hostess.

It would be the only time in Kimmi's life that she would hang on to herself.

I wasn't any more stable, had no idea how to balance food or emotions. Small portions made me feel unloved. Anorexia was on the rise and I kept getting bigger. I had a grease tooth, lived on fast food. It made me break out. A dermatologist diagnosed me with a condition called "McDonald's Acne."

Bingeing and restrictions helped to numb feelings of guilt, depression and shame. That day at Ruffage, Richard Simmons had put his arm around me like a concerned father and said, "I've been watching you. You're very attractive but you need to lose ten pounds now before it becomes twenty. And it will."

Why was everything a mixed message? Why did we all have to *Think Thin* to be considered desirable? Worthy? It would take years for me to learn to treat myself with gentleness, compassion and finally, self-love.

By 1990, the average age a girl started dieting had dropped to eight years old.

Kimmi managed to stay skinny her whole life. She never did pose for *Playboy*. It was Candy Loving who'd win the Great Playmate Hunt in '79. But Dorothy Stratten would become *Playboy*'s shiniest star, pegged as "the next Marilyn Monroe," appearing in their August issue and as Playmate of the Year in 1980.

It scares me how much she resembled Kimmi. They could have been twins.

Stratten would lose her life at twenty to all of the beautiful ugly things that make this place L.A. She was ensnared, long before she was murdered.

As for Kimmi, she was delicate as a hybrid tea rose, fragile, broken in the box. When we were girls, I wanted to be her, but when I realized that would never happen, I tried to save her.

Kimmi was too consumed with feelings of inadequacy to find any true happiness. She battled depression, an eating disorder, a series of bad relationships and drug addiction. At forty two, she jumped seventeen stories off a balcony in Marina del Rey.

There was always this part of me, call it my core, an inner strength, a knowing that I would be okay no matter what. There was always this part of her, call it *her* core: a knowing that she would never feel safe, never find love, never soar.

Her lingering essence both comforts and haunts me. Her absence, a reminder of my presence. And I have never felt so close to anyone, before or since.

LOST EXPLORERS

The Family Table

Jewish tradition recognizes a meal as a time for intimacy, fellowship, and significant conversation.
— Rabbi Yehiel E. Poupko, Judaic Scholar

Dinnertime was when we talked about the future. Advice for living was dispensed like slogans from commercials: "If unique is what you seek." "Hang in there, Baby." *"Be somebody. Not a nobody."*

During these discussions, it became clear that I wasn't going to be a lawyer or a judge, a newscaster, private detective or an actress in a Woody Allen movie. I wasn't outstanding in any field. Somewhere along the way, I got the unspoken message: "Find a man to take care of you. Men come first."

My parents loved me, I never doubted that. But I wasn't their project. They relied on school to form me. Ballet? Disco dancing class? Theatre Club? Those came from friends who invited me in.

I carried an assumption that I wasn't capable of finding and taking care of myself. So I created a role I could get behind, one that made me feel like I had a superpower: taking care of everyone else.

If I Follow You Home…Will You Keep Me?
(from an iron-on patch on my overalls)

When I was nineteen, my heart had a head-on collision with a once-famous matinee idol, twenty-five years my senior. He had the boots, the breath, the space in his step. He had the rugged, feelingless behavior. I was still living at home with my parents when I met Wayne Maunder. Every night, my friends and I would drive forty minutes to West Hollywood to hang out on the patio of Joe Allen. It was like Schwab's in the dark, only fancier, the West Coast branch of an East Coast theatre-vortex for actors in the 80s, where all of the greats and the not-so-greats could be found drinking, dining or waiting tables. Anything was better than socializing at a coffee shop on Ventura Boulevard and calling it a nightlife. At Joe Allen, we felt like escape artists.

The place was decorated with posters of Broadway flops. Wayne held court there with a group of middle-aged-plus, coffee-drinking character actors. They'd sit for hours, this *Broadway Danny Rose*-type clan, regaling each other with tales of auditions, near misses and a handful of hits. They were thespians, directors, filmmakers, most of whom were flat broke and incredibly cocky. There was Lenny, Michael, Eric, Robert and others whose names I can't remember. Each had his own sad story about gaining success and watching as it slipped away. And in a couple cases, returning.

They would check out and rank every ingénue parading through the room and weren't so gracious, unless you were a looker. The waitresses despised them, would take their nominal tips and tolerate their pre-Me Too humor. One of the guys lured aspiring actresses up to his duplex, claiming he was a photographer. He would guarantee them modeling work, pretend to be taking "artistic pictures," get them to take their tops off (and other things) and afterwards, berate these girls to the other guys at the table because he'd shot them with no film in his camera.

Then there was Wayne, who would always make an effort to stop and talk with me. He was the most gorgeous man I'd ever seen. He knew it. And he used it. He was detached, glib, wry. He glowed in the dark. He'd dreamed of being a major league baseball player but failed in tryouts and became a TV star instead. He peaked in the late 60s and early 70s with three TV series: *Custer, Lancer* and *Chase*. He'd been on the cover of TV Guide, twice. When we met, he was having a minor comeback after years of unemployment, had just completed a role in the movie *Porky's*. It was a runaway hit, an unexpected #1 and he was sparkling, getting newfound attention, a second wind.

"Why do you dress like that?" he'd ask, referring to the aggressive shoulder pads and designer sweatshirt dresses I favored, courtesy of Norma Kamali. "Why do you wear so much fucking makeup? You look like a clown at a children's party. Show your real face. Let yourself be natural. You'd look a helluva lot better."

He was forty-four, living in a rental on Elm Drive in Beverly Hills with his thirteen year old son, Dylan. Years earlier, he'd had a wife who'd lost her mind and moved back to her family in New York, making him an instant, full-time father.

He invited me over, asked me all kinds of questions about myself like he was interested and was a good listener. Then he pulled out his guitar and played, "You've Got to Hide Your Love Away." At the end of our evening, he walked me to my car he said, "You carry yourself like you're trying to hide a secret. Stand proud, even if you're not."

I would call Wayne every day and we'd meet for coffee at The Bread Winner on Beverly Drive or for lunch at Old World Restaurant or Mirabelle on Sunset and partake in what he called "laughing and scratching." Late at night, we'd reconnect for sex and sleeping. He wasn't a good lover. His maxim was, "Every man for himself." So, it became a cozy pattern more than a hot romance.

Wayne was a throwback to another era. He called women "broads." Held the power. I felt powerless and drawn in, wanting the next phase of my life to begin. I glommed on, felt protective of his son, like a big sister to him. Dylan and I were only five and a half years apart. I made sure I became indispensable to both of them.

The aging actor pals Wayne sat with at Joe Allen called me "The Kid." Wayne seemed to agree with them. "You remind me of Shirley Temple in a movie I saw thirty-five years ago. *The Bachelor and the Bobby-Soxer*. It's about a teenaged girl named Susan who gets fleeting crushes on an assortment of inappropriate suitors, until she meets an indifferent older man, Cary Grant, whom she doggedly pursues. Only in the movie, they don't end up together..."

Juvenescence

He couldn't get arrested after Porky's *and within a year, Wayne was flat broke and he and Dylan were about to be evicted. I had just turned twenty, started making my own money as a daytime waitress at Café Figaro and I rented an apartment in Westwood for the three of us. Wayne had a bad credit score. My father was the co-signer on the lease.*

Dylan got the bedroom and Wayne and I slept in the living room: me on the couch, Wayne in a sleeping bag on the floor. On a good night, we got the floor together.

He could explode over nothing, take it all out on me. Punch walls, kick in doors. When he went back to being a waiter and a bartender, he blamed me for the demise of his career.

I would retaliate by sleeping with other men behind his back. I'd make sure to be home by the end of his shift. He'd hand me a bundle of cash and I'd count his tips for him, sort it all into neat piles on the dining room table.

When I wasn't around, Dylan would ask him, "Why do YOU get all the girls?"

Her Life as a Sad Country Love Song

(a cheating ballad)

He was a poor man's Kris Kristofferson, cowboy style with a Seventies edge: wedge of grey beard/voice of gravel/Lee jeans; long and lean with a belly and breath like whiskey, smoke, beer and dirt, torn Western shirt from the Union Rescue Mission, where he'd stay when it came time for eviction.

She was a Valley Girl in skin and bone, had her own Trimline pushbutton phone since she was ten; a rich man's daughter in her own mind. Designer clothes charged to credit cards, five-dollar housefrau dresses from thrift stores, scores of made to look worn out boots, an indication to the world at large that she'd lived some.

At the Coronet Pub, where she would go to write and he would go to drink, she found him one night chain-smoking Tareytons and strumming a nylon stringed guitar. And she listened at the bar while he sang "Beautiful Brown Eyes" in her honor.

Her boyfriend mixed drinks for a living around the corner at the Raincheck Room. He was a once-known, now unknown movie star with a flashy car and a hair-trigger temper. He still had his looks, was well preserved, only with an axe to grind for finding himself permanently out of the loop and relegated to wages.

She was a wannabe ingénue of sorts: waitress job as last resort/acting class/the rare audition. She sucked. Everyone told her to quit and be a writer, so she'd sit in dark bars and scribble-scrabble, then head back to the West Hollywood shack, where once she'd had lots of sex turned into no sex with the Raincheck bartender.

They'd lived this way for years, parallel parked and sometimes intersected. Staying out 'til dawn, sleeping 'til Noon, frequenting local cafes in the late afternoon where they'd scour the want ads, make lists of goals on legal pads then read them back to each other. Lists of goals made them feel purposeful.

Still, she was alone in the world and she knew it, and the guy with cowboy style at the Coronet made her feel less so. He was a Vietnam vet who'd been sprayed with Agent Orange. He was legendary as a barroom fixture and for making scenes, and known for coming clean when he'd drink, which was always.

He was missing a finger that he'd lost in a fight. Under a cracked La Cienega streetlight, he let her touch the stump, then touched her cheek for good measure. He was a limo driver by trade, he said, and invited her to visit him in the parking lot of the Beverly Hills Hotel, where Dav El kept the stretches.

When she appeared the following day, they lay tucked away in an empty limo and he kissed her. She closed her eyes and pretended that they were in the backseat, not the front, pretended that she was Barbra Streisand and he was Kris Kristofferson in the remake of *A Star Is Born,* singing "Lost Inside of You."

That night in his friend's Murphy bed, instead of making out they snuggled, while he drank can after can of Old Milwaukee and sang softly in her ear. She could taste the beer in the sweat dripping from his face and it reminded her of a tired horse after the race or rain drying on a screen door. What's more, his blankets were coarse, Salvation Army green.

She gave him her headshot upon request and while they were both still undressed, he gave her a work tape of original songs mostly about existential longing and destitution. He said he loved her more than his so-called Nashville dream and that the best and worst memories he'd ever seen were of war.

She imagined her life as a sad country love song. She already had the outfit. Long curling-ironed hair, ruffled floral dress and an oversized tiger's eye ring. How she loved to listen to him sing: hillbilly boogie, honky-tonk, the Bakersfield sound, rockabilly swing.

A man who'd drink and come clean, read *Horsemanship* magazine and practice roping on a plastic supermarket steer, his fledgling career and half-baked heart right out of the pages of a Sam Shepard play, like the one she'd been rehearsing for days in acting class.

But the men in most country songs and western style plays, the ones that look so good onstage, fall apart from their own sense of rage and that magnetic pull towards doom: their desert motel room, a prison of whiskey, smoke, beer and dirt; wedge of grey beard/voice of gravel/ Lee jeans/torn Western shirt.

Culmination Proceedings

> *Well, he musta had a screw loose, in his head*
> *To end up like this after all he said.*
> — Dave Alvin

Wayne listened to Ray Charles and Nat King Cole.
He would sing to me.
Our song was "Unforgettable."
We were together for nearly seven years.
He called himself my "bridge from childhood to adulthood."
Tore me down and taught me how to stand up for myself.
Urged me into womanhood and independence.
I emerged and outgrew him.
But he shaped me into what Cat Stevens called a "Hard Headed Woman."
When we split, he moved to the Valley, and I was the co-signer of his lease.

"I'm just a visiting savage," he would say. And perhaps he was.

A Legacy Act

Shortly after we broke up, I was reading TV Guide *when I saw that somebody had written in, asking: "Whatever happened to Wayne Maunder?"*

His biggest moment would come in 2019, when Quentin Tarantino included him as a real life and fictional character in his feature film, Once Upon A Time in Hollywood. *Luke Perry would play Wayne's former character "Scott" in the TV show* Lancer *and the actor "Wayne Maunder."*

Both Luke and Wayne would die before the movie was released.

The Game of Belief
(1989)

I used to be a believer,
believed in the voodoo of mortal witches,
the power of myth and incantation
in everyday existences,
total honesty
at the cost of losing
a potential friend or lover
and in monogamy
at the cost of losing you.
I believed in the geometry of surrender,
the cadence of ash
and in the commonality
of domestic vaudeville acts.
I believed in the geography
of sacrifice and bliss,
the histrionics of self-deception
and fighting for inner peace
until I became an activist
in my own war of remembrance
and lost.
I believed in the low cost of simple tasks
performed daily
though they negated the cause and effect,
the natural process—
the faith of blind men
who could still see me
and the clarity of those
who couldn't.
Maybe all that I've given up over the years
is a game I must re-learn.

He Called Himself a Very Late Bloomer

Was Harry Dean Stanton good friends with every woman I knew?

He definitely touched my life, but only once, and it was nothing he would have ever remembered and something I'll never forget. I wasn't a starlet-type, certainly not his type, but when we met, he was gentle and attentive to me and that was life-changing. It was 1985 when I went with my friend Lori and her girlfriend Darlene to hear him sing love songs, mostly in Spanish, at McCabe's Guitar Shop in Santa Monica. Darlene was close with him and mentioned to us that she'd consider having him father her child.

That night, Madonna was there with Sean Penn. This was right around the time she was becoming one of the biggest pop stars in the world. She and Sean, recently married, were lightning bugs; glistening and out of place in the unassuming crowd of folkies. The two of them sat together in the folding seats of the front row of McCabe's, as Harry Dean played guitar and sang songs that he would dedicate to their new love.

After the concert, Lori, Darlene and I drove across town to Helena's on Temple Street, where we had been invited by Harry Dean. When we got there, he was sitting in a booth with Madonna and Sean, who ignored us, even though we'd been asked by Harry Dean to come sit with them.

I was insecure in those days, feeling like I wasn't important enough for them to say "Hi." And I wasn't. And they didn't. The only person who talked to me in that club was Harry Dean. I got to sit next to him and hear his simple but ancient wisdom, his quotes from Chief Seattle, about "this web of life" and "not leaving footprints," about how there's "no death, only a change in worlds." He rambled on and I was all ears. This conversation ended up inspiring me to create a character like him in a play I would eventually write.

I'd seen his tremendous talent as an actor in *Paris, Texas* and in numerous other films, including the best one, *Straight Time*. I remember him singing "Just a Closer Walk with Thee" and playing guitar in *Cool Hand Luke*. He was very well known but he wasn't an icon yet. He was Tops in my book. What struck me that night at McCabe's—watching Harry Dean interpreting these old-time ballads, not as a character in someone else's film, but playing himself—was his tenderness.

When in the booth at Helena's, he gave me his full attention. I didn't mention his acting roles or that I even knew who he was, but told him how much the songs he'd performed had moved me, particularly "Annabel Lee," an adaptation of the Edgar Allan Poe poem about true love transcending death. He started singing it, a cappella, right there in a private concert for one.

I confessed how shy and out of place I felt, told him I didn't like being in crowded bars where I didn't know anyone or at nightclubs around celebrities, that it made me uncomfortable, made me want to run away. He put his hand on my shoulder, looked deep into my eyes and said, "Honey, if you're centered, you can be anywhere." Then Madonna pulled him away, dragged him out to the dance floor. She was doing most of the dancing and whispering in his ear.

Afterwards, he returned to the same spot where he'd been sitting, next to me. He wasn't flirting or making moves, it wasn't that sort of an exchange. He was calm and knowing and I felt like I could say anything to him and he wouldn't think less of me.

In spite of his words about being centered, which I didn't understand at the time, I couldn't handle being at Helena's. I didn't belong there, so I told Lori and Darlene I wanted to leave. I said goodbye to Harry Dean and thanked him for all the poetic insight he'd shared. And he wrote down his phone number and home address and said, "If you want to talk again, I'm here for you."

But he had turned into a superstar of sorts. And when I'd think about calling him, he seemed out of reach.

When he died more than thirty years from that night, I was sorry I never had the courage to call him or drive over there to continue the conversation. I sure could have used some more of his advice.

Raymond Carver is Haunting the Topanga Ranch Motel

And then I met a memoirist. He was electrifying, empathetic, unpretentious.

I put on a full-fledged Dog and Pony show just for him. I paid for the rented room. He'd said that where sex was concerned, it was all about giving permission.

For someone who wrote the truth of his life, he wasn't so candid. Mostly we talked about books. He was reading Love in the Time of Cholera *and telling me about the emotional significance of eggplant. I was reading* What We Talk About When We Talk About Love.

He didn't want to talk about love. He said he didn't adore me but he respected me. He told me my strength was in my enthusiasm.

He said my belly was "like a third breast."

Wormhole

Another flashing chance at bliss.
— The Doors

I was in search of those things you can't get back, like faith, like old photographs, before it all fades into an outline, a skeleton of your original intention. I wanted to recapture what drew me in in the first place: open arms of acceptance, the oath of understanding, a slide show of my parents, dancing slow and easy to "The Crystal Ship" *as I watched them from behind the doorway, trusting.*

LANDED

Floodlights

I found Christopher Allport onstage in a Pinter play at the Mark Taper Forum and announced to my dearest friend, Pattie: "That's the man I'm going to spend the rest of my life with." Nothing had ever been clearer.

We met during an after-show celebration, where Chris barely spoke. A friend who'd co-starred in the play said he could see us together, but Chris was in the wreckage of a dissolving marriage and couch hopping. This friend offered to pass my number on to him and called the next week to say, "Chris wants you to have his number too."

Neither of us reached out.

Three months later, Chris showed up at Poetry in Motion on a night when I was reading. We were seated right across from each other and he remembered me from our first meeting, and flipped out over the poem I read. He suggested we "write a song together."

On our second date, he blurted out, "I feel like I could spend thirty years with you." I remember thinking, "Why not fifty?"

He was the domesticated wild man I'd been searching for. He wore fleece year-round and EVERYONE wanted to touch him.

Butterfly and Moth

He said, "Here's my problem: Either I feel nothing or I feel everything."
"Which category do I fall into?" I asked. "Wait, don't tell me."
"You're a butterfly. You make me feel alive inside."

No one had ever said things like that and it didn't seem real.

My last and only long-term love clearly stated that I'd ruined his life, stolen his wild.
I'd taken his word for it, believing I had that much power.

Then he said, "I'm a moth. I rest with my wings open."

I moved to his side of the booth to get a sense of how he felt, up close and fluttering.
His breath, not his words, filled the air. I could feel its heat as it traveled from his
mouth on a relief journey, a carbon dioxide ride that evaporated on my cheeks. I
could feel the filmy mist of human fog.

The Original Home
(*1990*)

We had never seen each other in the daylight. All our dates had been at night in places like dark movies. That first morning together, a Santa Barbara new moon forced a getaway to a Zen monastery, where weather determined one's point of reflection, where they used kerosene lamps instead of electric light. We felt closer to the stars, even with the waking of an early sun.

Half the fun was reinforcing the fact that opposites do attract. Even at sea level, we were the two poles, everywhere but our tentative hearts, re-living the road trip of Kerouac on Robinson Jeffers' Big Sur sand where we read Rilke aloud. He sang western stories and played a Taylor guitar. We wrote our own country ballad in the car. He called me "Bonnie," so I just had to call him "Clyde." Drank Bailey's from the bottle, made up names to call our imaginary baby. On this small-town meditation spree, I confessed that the forest was a new idea for me.

Hiking off-trail in the Tassajara rocks, I lost my footing, and he told me: "Trust the Earth more, that's what it's there for, to keep our feet rooted to the original home." We were carved in stone or covered wagon people in that painting of the American West, Charles Russell's best, called "When The Land Belonged To God." But these surroundings were surreal. I rested between the trees, took in the ease of water that ran under us as if it made its own decisions with the liberation of natural things.

Spread out bare-boned and open with sack lunch clenched between milk-fed thighs, I felt alive in the ancient northern ruins, primitive and free like the apogee, as I watched his reflection in the mineral baths he faced, encased between a winding stream called The Narrows and big white rocks shaped as if for human forms.

It was then that I started to fall for him, while he slept naked and exposed, resembling that terracotta sculpture of Jupiter's head and his body, an archaic outer landscape of water and clay only with the modern-day damage of a weekend mountain climber. The cuts and jags were mementos of Mount Shasta and Idyllwild, where he once fell forty feet and caught his face on the rope, with the hope of surviving long enough to reach the rock's potential—and his own.

I photographed the demography of radiance, the glory of being—each curve of his face a secret prayer, each crack and line a scripture to live by. It was then that I knew full well that the truest of beauty came not from the shelter of the indoors I have known but from being alone in centuries of debris. His soul was dry dirt mixed with stone, his feet fixed to the Earth, The Original Home.

Darby Slick Was on to Something

He was a Connecticut Yankee with a Christian name, a child of the Sixties and a win-win compared to the sincere California liars I'd previously attached myself to, the ones who'd assisted in ensnaring me into a perpetual state of discontent and ecstasy.

He was Hi-Lo, a cross between the Colony Club on the Upper East Side and the Speak Easy Cocktail Bar on Pico in Santa Monica.

He played guitar with a harmonica holder around his neck, wrote his own songs, sounded like Jim Croce and Harry Chapin, had tears in his throat.

He told me he'd come close to being "a big star," that he'd acted in almost a hundred television shows, guesting or recurring. He said he was "on the precipice, in a good way."

He was a relationship person and the father of a ten year old boy. He'd never been without a woman. He wanted "Somebody to Love." He needed "Somebody to Love." I was drawn to his want, to his need. It gave him a refreshing quality. Even with a familiar hotheadedness, he was a breather from the poseurs.

I decided to marry him then, and tortured myself with the plague of all interfaith unions: Who would perform the ceremony? A priest? A rabbi? Or both?

He Didn't Even Call Me a Klutz

The first time Chris took me to the snow, I fell and broke my wrist —on the way to my cross-country ski lesson. He was telemarking in the backcountry, with no idea that ski patrol had come to my aid and transported me to Mammoth Hospital, where an emergency room doctor re-broke the bone and put me in a short arm cast.

I took a taxi back to Tamarack Lodge. Chris ran outside, beaming. "How was your day in the powder? I imagine you've been loving every second of it!"

His Voice
for Andrew

We were eating Godmothers in my red jeep. This would be our first time alone, me and my future stepson. He liked his sub with the bread hot, loaded with Italian meats: capocollo, mortadella, Genoa salami, ham and prosciutto della mamma. I liked mine vegetarian, provolone with the works: mayonnaise, mustard, onions, lettuce, tomatoes and extra pickles.

He was ten. His parents had split a few months back. He'd witnessed their fighting, his father's capacity for rage but there's no way, at his age, he could understand the complexity of their break-up.

His father was with *me* now yet still trying to win his wife back.

And there I was at twenty seven, with another young son of another compelling, half-available man with an anger issue, another actor who'd wanted to be a household name, another one raised by wolves with no rules, no guidelines, too much charisma and an imagined license to spew.

In the parking lot of Bay Cities on Lincoln Boulevard in Santa Monica, we ate in silence, listening to KRTH-101. "Rocky Raccoon" came on. At the time it seemed like a long song. I found out it was only three and a half minutes. My future stepson knew every word, sang boldly as if onstage performing for an audience. He had a bittersweet, emotional voice with perfect pitch that came straight from his core. He was alchemized when singing.

When the song was over, we opened the Zapp's and there was mostly crunching. We washed it all down with IBC and I told him, "You should be a singer when you grow up."

He replied, "She doesn't want him back but you're still in a triangle."

My Nature
(journal entry 1991)

I found my place
in the mountains.
I bake, turn on the heat,
look out the window,
take pictures of trees.
When people ask me what I do here,
I tell them, "I'm base camp.
I keep the cabin warm."

Animals Like Us

I grow with you, sprout roots, prepare
for battles, celebrate victories,
study the mechanics of your inadequacy,
reverberation of my need.
Our bed ignites as if it has been heated
by a warming pan: hyperkinetic, oppositional.
My pigtails electric, in preparation
for a rural manifesto.
This is not the gravy train
but a cow town to live in for a stretch,
where you are wrinkle-free at seventy
and I am fifty-five with long gray hair
and legions of ethnic jewelry.
Our bed is Greek fire, incendiary,
just like the Byzantines planned for it
to burst into flames upon wetness.
This barn dance has no ending.
We culminate in square roots
to the beat of *Oklahoma* and *Annie Get Your Gun.*
The numerology adds up to equal.
I have been afflicted with the limited audience
of this beast epic: as long as I keep walking
barefoot against the calm of your chest,
deceased or delinquent,
always a tongue of light with you.

The Yiddish Word for Destiny

> *It lies not in our power to love, or hate*
> *For will in us is over-rulde by fate.*
> — Christopher Marlowe

When I told my father that Chris had proposed, he said, "You don't marry an actor."
When I told my mom, she said, "You don't marry a man who hates his mother."

At the rehearsal dinner. Dad raised his glass to make a toast: "Welcome to the
family. We love you, but don't take our daughter with you on your wild adventures."

After, the machatunim *regrouped in the lobby of San Ysidro Ranch, where we*
were to be married the next day. My father pulled me aside, walked me into the hotel's
study. He picked up a book, Hero and Leander *and handed me a page he'd torn*
from it, a Christopher Marlowe poem: "Who Ever Lov'd, that Lov'd Not at
First Sight?"

"Reminds me of the night you met. How you just knew. It was beshert,*" he said.*

Conceived

Think I'm gonna have a son.
— Kenny Loggins

When our child Mason was born, there was a clearing in my heart, simple as a snow plowed road after a massive storm. I named him after a singing waiter I'd met when I was twelve, a Kenny Loggins doppelgänger who'd worked at The Great American Food and Beverage Company in Santa Monica.

Allan Mason had dedicated "Danny's Song" to me and I'd never forgotten it— or him.

Convert

Chris was more Jewish than I was.
Insisted on lighting the Hanukkah candles.
Made better latkes than Rabbi Schulweis' wife.
Didn't know how to fix anything around the house.
Asked to join a Temple.
Read Elie Wiesel.
Was obsessed with Jackie Mason.
Wanted to nail a mezuzah to our doorway.
Did everything short of getting circumcised.

A Poet's Guide to Hot Springs of the West

Most weekends, we didn't make plans with other families.
Chris would load us into his truck and we would head out
to Lone Pine, Independence, Bishop, Mammoth or
29 Palms. I wasn't into camping, so we'd trade off. One night
in the open air. Another in a cozy motel. Fancy hotels were
for when he was working on a TV show and someone else
was paying. Wherever we went, we never missed hitting a river,
lake, mud bath or hot spring: Wild Willy's, Dr. Wilkinson's,
Deep Creek, Harbin, Benton, Sespe, Wilbur. Chris would
undress in front of anyone and soak endlessly.

He had this idea:

"Let's invite our favorite poets. Michael C Ford, Scott Wannberg,
S.A. Griffin, Michael Lally, Holly Prado, Harry Northup,
Eve Brandstein, Laurel Ann Bogen. We'll get a VW van, or
caravan to different hot springs on a road trip from California
to Wyoming, get everyone to undress, wade in the healing waters
then write poems about it. We'll turn it into an anthology, edited by
you and me. It'll be a bestseller. Who wouldn't want to read it?"

Amblyopia

My husband had a wandering eye. At first, I thought he was checking out other women but then I realized it was physiological, he had poor depth perception and an imbalance in his eye muscle.

I think it's the reason he never had the acting career he'd wished for: with the looks of a leading man, he kept getting cast as a character actor. That wandering eye gave him mystery and danger, there was something a little "off" about him, his eyes didn't work together, he could never fix his gaze.

Leaving the eye untreated for most of his life damaged his overall vision. When he wasn't wearing contact lenses, he wore coke-bottle glasses. Without either, he was practically blind.

And then he got Lasik. I thought, this will be the end of our marriage. I'd always been one big blur. But I quickly learned the naked art of backing out of a room.

ENDANGERED

Inherited

My father started losing so much weight, out of nowhere. He acted like everything was okay, wore the same pants, belted more tightly.

I worked at his office in Century City: answering phones, light accounting, updating supplements. In between these menial tasks, I would write. One afternoon, I stayed late to complete a story and moved into the library of his suite.

He walked in to say something. We were both drinking protein shakes: his, a banana almond smoothie from his health club, Century West; mine, a can of SlimFast, He started hiccupping. He couldn't stop. He was embarrassed but he didn't leave the room.

When he caught his breath he said, "You can have it, you know. It's the perfect place for a writer. I want to give you this library."

Gross Negligence

Now he was in a coma. He'd survived all-day surgery for what turned out to be cancer of the esophagus. He was aware and awake but then they pulled out his breathing tube too soon. There was a Code Blue. No one thought to do a trach. He was left without oxygen for eleven minutes.

It was a resident's fault. Part of the training was to work seventy-two hours without sleep.

He was unresponsive, on a ventilator and a feeding tube for two months. Our family didn't want to let him go. His color was good, he was gaining weight and when I was in the room alone with him, it was as if he could hear me, like he was listening. His blood pressure would go down when he'd hear my voice.

The O.J. trial had begun, was on the overhead TV in his hospital room for weeks.

When we'd arrive at the hospital first thing in the morning, we'd find the nurses sitting in the visitors' chairs, hooked to the television screen. Johnny Cochran made his opening statement for the defense. I watched Denise Brown testify that her sister was an abused wife.

I brought in a boombox and played him the songs he most loved: "My Favorite Year" by Michael Feinstein, the entire soundtrack from *Phantom of the Opera*. I wanted to wake him, I wanted to buoy him up.

Everything on him kept growing. Like someone who was healthy. His fingernails needed clipping. His beard begged for a trimming. He was a tidy man. Distinguished. Impeccable. He'd had a legendary beard that he paid a beautician to trim once a week. Now he was starting to look like Howard Hughes.

I brought a clippers and a scissors from home, pulled them from my purse. First I cut and filed his nails. Then my mom and I took turns trimming his beard. We did a horrible job. It was ragged.

I realized in my whole life as his daughter, I had never once touched my father's beard. He was untouchable, until he wasn't.

The World of Sleep

What was he thinking, if anything? Was he flooded by silent movies of his lifetime?

When he was three in the West Side of Chicago and his mother left him in his white suit on the fence outside their house, told him to sit there and wait, forgetting about him for hours until she remembered him and returned, to find him in the same spot?

How he almost died of thyroid cancer right after he married my mom?

Did he remember that day we went to Pink's, where we had a hot dog eating contest and tied, having eaten six each?

Or when he took me to Yamato for a tempura feast and we left our shoes at the entrance and when we finished, discovered both pairs had been stolen, forcing us to walk back to his office barefoot?

Did he know one of the doctors botched the job? That none of them had used the word "brain-dead"?

Book of Bargains

I was born at this same hospital, the one that killed my father. They billed my family over a million dollars for a medical crisis they created. We settled out of court for a nominal amount to avoid a trial we would probably have lost, since juries are known to side with doctors in medical malpractice lawsuits.

When I was little, I could never pronounce this hospital's name, would tell people that I was "from Sears—my parents purchased me from a catalog."

Sweet Tooth

(from my eulogy)

My father was a "leg" man. On his 60ᵗʰ birthday, he'd asked me to buy him a woman's thigh made of chocolate from Godiva in Beverly Hills. They were sold out, so I bought him a semi-sweet telephone instead. He would call me from his real phone, the rotary, and say, "I'm working on the dial center now" or "I've just finished off the receiver."

Starstruck
for Shikey

I was six years old and having lunch at the Farmer's Market on Fairfax with my father when he pointed out a small, round man in a dark overcoat. He was wearing a tilted grey fedora, sitting on a bench, drinking coffee and smoking a cigar. "See that guy? He's the most acclaimed movie star in the whole world. Go ask him for his autograph!"

Edward G. Robinson was perched in the vicinity of DuPar's. He looked like many of the other older actors who congregated there. Only he was by himself, with that faraway look in his eyes and a hard shell around him, to ward off lookie-loos. I had no idea who he was, felt embarrassed and shy about approaching him, but my father persisted, wouldn't take "No" for an answer.

"Excuse me, Mr. Robinson. May I have your autograph?" I asked.

"Why sure, young lady. And who shall I make this out to?" he inquired, scanning the area for someone much closer to his age who surely would have recognized him and wanted his valuable signature. He found my father leaning against the wall of DuPar's, trying to act nonchalant. He locked eyes with him, shook his head and grimaced. Then he smiled at me, tore off a piece of paper from his placemat and wrote, "For Suzy. With every good wish, Edward G. Robinson."

On the drive back home to the Valley, my father's voice was trembling with glee and wonder. "Put that away, somewhere safe. It's worth thousands of dollars. He's Jewish, y'know. From Romania, like your grandparents. His real name is Emanuel Goldenberg. But those in the know call him Manny."

I lost the autograph, but when I married Chris, we would watch Edward G. Robinson movies at home together on the VHS and I would wish my father had been alive so I could tell him that his favorite actor had become the one I most admired. I wish I could tell him that I have never witnessed a more captivating presence onscreen, that there wouldn't be a Brando, Nicholson, De Niro or Pacino without him.

And every time I go to the Farmer's Market, I look over at that table and can still spot Eddie G.—I mean Manny—huddled in his own world, not wanting to be seen. He's been gone since 1973 but he is always there. And I can feel my father, who is also absent and yet ever-present. He's been gone since 1995 but his dignity and strength remain a blanket of protection, his sense of invisible magic, something I forever will be seeking.

NOWHERE TO BE FOUND

Paris 2003

'Cause you don't know where life takes you
Car tu ne sais pas où la vie t'amène
—Françoise Hardy/Michel Berger

Flushed with the energy of art and alliance
the rocket science of materia prima
he takes me by the hand to wisteria and secrets
steals my breath and kisses me
like I'm his new mistress, not his old wife.

This is our life and love is earned
sealed with an alchemist's loyalty
and candlewax from sticky long nights
of burning.

Singular as a field holler
a worn-out blues tune written for us alone
yet universal in skin and bone,
his attendance, his inscription
a hermetic cabinet of curiosities
called Home.

The Boulevard glows with our footprints
stable and so slippery.
Walking on ice has never been this easy.
Hang on.
Witness. Heartbeat. Godsend.
Any minute this could end.

The Tower (XVI) Upright

The week before it happened, I went to the Psychic Eye in Sherman Oaks on a whim. The reader, Clarissa, asked me to shuffle the deck and pull a single tarot card.

She held it up and said, "Soooo. You're a widow."

I swore to her I'd been married to the same man for a hundred years. I shoved my wedding ring in her face. It was three karats, had belonged to my mom, was a luminous nightlight in her dimly lit room.

"Well, your husband, he's off in his cave. He just has to go off, doesn't he?"

Then she stopped talking and started listening to the voices in her head.

"You've picked La Maison Dieu, a Major Arcana card. See the spire on top of the rocky mountain being struck by lightning? With fireballs and two people blasted out, falling to their deaths? Brace yourself."

Now You Are a Missing Person

1.

There is no waiting required
when reporting a person who is missing.
The Department of Justice makes it easy.

Without a copy of your fingerprints,
dental records, skeletal x-rays;
without a photo of what you look like

I fill out the form as next-of-kin,
pretend the essential information
will help find you—alive.

That's when I realize,
for all the chances you take
you have never broken a bone.

My hand will not stop shaking.
A volunteer tells me:
"Millions of Americans suffer from anxiety."

2.

Every month your magazine,
Rock and Ice, arrives in the mail.
You read the OBITUARY section first.

I know from being your wife
that climbers and free-heel skiers
rarely die of heart failure,

old age or terminal illness.
You are unaffected by expired Sherpas.
It's the everyday alpinists that get to you.

"Death by slab avalanche," you announce.
The very idea makes you sweat, makes you smell
like a barbequed beef sandwich.

I'm reading the latest issue of *Vogue*:
Street Style. Trends. Images of the Week.
I dog-ear the page, prepare for more.

3.

"I knew the guy. A bonehead. A wuss.
It could have been prevented.
But then, there are many worse ways to die."

Filling out the Missing Person form,
I feel accompanied by all your dead acquaintances,
the ones that make you feel superior.

My hand will not stop shaking.
I want to ask, How could you vanish
on a mountain of man-made snow?

I want to scream: Come home!
as rescuers search ungroomed trails,
as helicopters and newscasters hover.

But your future *Rock and Ice* obituary
has already been written.
A coroner's truck circles the parking lot.

But What About Odetta?

our son asked,
when I told him
his father was missing
in the snow.
She was his favorite singer,
this was to be her final tour.
She was seventy-seven.
He was eleven.
We had tickets to see her
in concert that night,
had been planning it
for months.
He cried when I told him
we couldn't go.

Our son was used to
his father taking off
to the woods
or the rocks,
some river or slope.
He could be late,
get lost sometimes
or snowed in
but he'd always find us
and catch up to whatever
we had planned.

Our son asked if his father
could just meet us
at McCabe's
when he got home.
But I had to say "No,
this is more serious."
I needed to drive
to Mountain High
while listening to
car-radio news updates.
I needed to wait there

for my husband,
for his father
to be found,
one way or the other.

Our son asked,
when I got home,
if he could sleep
in the bed with me.
He knew they'd called off
the search
and his father was
still missing.
"When will he be back?"
he asked repeatedly.
I lit a candle,
turned out the lights.
From the bed,
when I looked up at
the ceiling,
I could have sworn
I'd seen the shadow
of a skier,
climbing uphill.

Our son was half-asleep
when I said,
"I don't have
a good feeling
about this."
I held him in my arms
for hours. Only
these days,
when he tells the story,
he doesn't even remember
my being there.
In the middle of the night,
I knelt in the kitchen
singing an Odetta song,
"Hit or Miss,"
trying to find comfort in

her rejoicing.
And finally, I stood over
the trash can,
tore up
the concert tickets.

John Muir Warned You This Could Happen

*...adventure is not made up of distant lands and mountaintops, rather, it lies in
one's own readiness to exchange the domestic hearth for an uncertain resting place.*
— Reinhold Messner

Some things you once read about him in a guidebook
have steered you to the quandary of this moment,
like how Muir believed a "forest of wilderness"
was the key to the universe, like how he said
"one should go to the woods for safety, if nothing else."

Now you are saddled to a glacier of imperfection,
a cross-section of city and country, field and stream;
a mountain man with a shelter dream, the quiddity of hubris.
And you think you belong to someone.
You write your story in indelible ink.

John Muir said he wanted to go "anywhere that was wild"
and here you are, in this naked swordfight of a marriage,
this willingness bond; a magic wand that speaks in tongues
with a dirty mouth, where sameness is your splintered rock,
where you unlock the trail map of a lifetime.

"The mountains are calling," Muir wrote. "And I must go."
Those very words echo from the one you love,
who resents The Father of National Parks —for sauntering.
Watch him! as he ambushes nature like a cat on a cricket.
Watch yourself as you pretend it isn't happening.

Remember that primer in your old guidebook,
The Responsibility Code?
About cartroads, signage and deep snow safety?
"Always stay in control. Keep away from closed areas."
But when you marry a man who builds quinzhees

with his bare hands: no compass, no beacon, off-piste,
making first tracks —while ignoring the watches, warnings,
the weather forecast. You're signing your life away
in invisible ink. You think you belong to someone.
You want to belong to someone.

You tell him, "John Muir walked a thousand miles
but he always came home."
He tells you, "You are not alone in my backcountry ways"
until he makes the smooth tele turns of his final run
and you find: You don't belong to anyone.

Souvenirs and Evidence

The Search and Rescue crew handed me the bag
like a forgotten sandwich. I held it for days;
a Zip-Loc of belongings: his taxi wallet, damp
from melted snow with twelve, crisp hundred-dollar bills,
weekend cash to pay for my 45th birthday.
His red bandana covered in rocks and ice,
smelling of sweat and torn mountain skin.
Our son's 5th grade picture in his wallet:
hazel eyes, pirate t-shirt, gypsy hair;
face staring back at me with that "I am safe" look.
And then the goggles, still foggy,
still defrosting from a long night and buried.
I held the bag for days; it was the last of him.
Later, when people came to pay their respects,
to tell me how he was in a better place,
"He died doing what he loved,"
only the ache remained,
like heart surgery without anesthesia.
I would share the bag and its contents
with anyone who was interested.
A friend put her arm around me and said:
"You don't have to worry anymore. All the things
you were afraid of have already happened to you."

Fight, Flight, Freeze, Fawn

When I pulled up to the drop-off line at school, my son got out of the car, dropped his notebook and backpack to the ground and sprinted from Euclid to Broadway to the alley. He would not stop running. I called the front office, begged for help. A few teachers came out, along with some parents. They chased and cornered him, gently restrained him, tried to talk him down. His limbs were flailing. He seemed impossible to contain.

I've lost them both, I thought.

Riven

At first, it felt like we were on a construction site and a crane fell from the sky and clobbered us on our heads. All our friends and strangers, too, came forward to hold our skulls together. I see that now, I'm the one who has to hold us up, without assistance.

Boys Without Fathers

This has always been
a "Quest" story:
adventures, magical rewards,
the tests

Running for my life
and from my life
since I had feet

running to meet
men
who were once
boys without fathers

They learned their way
around things,
not by choice
They've given voice
and reason
to my tiny little leaps
toward the Unknown

and I was (and still am)
prone,
susceptible
to their lack of guidance--
that moral (or immoral) code
invented
by being let loose
to draw conclusions
of their own

A father will reveal
a river's hidden moves;
the groove in the magic angle,
twenty degrees to skip a stone

not leave a boy
to bond with the Alone
and grow up overnight
with no instructions

A father will show
how to build a fire
pitch a tent
give directions
embellish all reflections

Fight with snowballs,
fish through ice
He'll be the one who says,
"Roll the dice,
it's your turn"

Your Turn

This has always been
a "Quest" story
with its circuitous route,
its point and its shoot,
its natural disasters

Still running to the men
who were once
boys without fathers

To seek from within them
what's unwritten:
the secret to dreaming
the unmarked trail
the backroad home
the way to make peace with the Alone

The adventures, the magical rewards,
the tests
and a plea in their honor,
a simple request:
Please teach me
how to grow my own boy,
the one without a Father.

To the Fairgrounds

I am waiting for your essence.
— Lucinda Williams

I went back to the Psychic Eye to see Clarissa for answers.

I told her, "One night he's lying next to me and the next week, his remains are in a plastic box. To think I used to wish for more closet space, more room to spread out, more things— when all you need are some old Levi's and a pair of good boots. All you need is the ability to reach your emergency contact."

She said, "He's within reach. I see him sitting around a bonfire at a carnival, afterhours, surrounded by your ancestors in the Eastern bloc. Instruments are being plucked. An array of woodwinds and strings. This assembly with him, they're nomads, Romani, of the 9th level and above. He's singing his heart out. They love him! The music, it's of the ancient kind: bolero, jazz, flamenco. The violin figures prominently. He's strumming— not a banjo or a guitar. I think it's a mandolin, yes, that's what he's playing. But he's calling it a 'mando.'"

"No way," I said. "That's what he called it. He bought one the week before he died. Went to Truetone Music, near the Third Street Promenade. Went back two or three times before he talked the price down. Only got to play that thing for seven days. I'm glad he gets to play it now."

The Broken Gift

In the Summer of 2004 we were in Nantucket for my mother-in-law's memorial. There was a gathering in her honor where we had to climb a ladder to get to the rooftop of someone's home and have drinks with other family members.

"Bet you've never been up on a Widow's Walk," Chris said. "Wives of mariners would stand on viewing platforms and await their husbands' return from the ocean, or not."

I remember thinking, I don't want to be up here. It's bad luck.

That's all I could think of four years later when I arrived at Our House Grief Support Center and stepped into a room of middle-aged grievers. I sat down and faced the others, each of whom had lost a spouse. There was nobody I wanted to be friends with. I truly thought my story was the worst story. No one's loss would be able to come close to mine.

Within minutes, it was as if we were all sewn together, a crazy quilt of inconsolables. My heart was excavated. Everyone's story was the worst story.

Meteorology

for Blue

And so I wonder
will I ever walk in snow again?
Begin to let go of the hand
of my frozen man
lured by powder and ice
enticed and betrayed by crystalline flakes.
Will I let another on the cracked lake
of my heart, reshaped and
newly landscaped by nature's perils?

It's Thanksgiving time
and the radio is playing Christmas carols.
I can smell last year's goose.
Am I right to save the Sorels,
the hand-knit scarves of prickly wool?
Full of life I am, and thankful.
I had no idea I had it all,
until now.
And how I have even more
of an awareness of what came before
the white-out conditions.

Ten Novembers ago,
we drove to a backcountry cabin
in a storm
kept snug by kerosene and skin on skin.
"Goodnight, I love you," we said again and again,
then fell into slumber under our winter coats.
By morning, he was reading Edward Abbey quotes
and teasing me about talking in my sleep.
"This time, I heard it and awoke
to the most beautiful word.
When you spoke, you said 'flurry.'"

Flurry: *a brief light snowfall*
the call of a sudden gust of wind
a stirring mass, as of leaves or dust,
a shower, a powerful burst of commotion,
a stir.

How could I have known we were
to be blown in different directions,
at the mercy of the atmosphere?

OTHERWISE MISSING

She said, "The Healing Meter Has Expired"

She said, "His death took the life out of you."
She said, "You used to be gracious and carefree."
She said, "You've lost all of your joy. And charisma."
She said, "Everyone is waiting for the happy ending to this story."
She said, "Stop asking about my art and calling it 'my art.'"
She said, "Now that you're single, your ego is out of control."
She said, "It's like you're on some power trip with men."
She said, "You used to treat me like I was magic."
She said, "Every conversation between us was an awakening."
She said, "I didn't like it when my husband called you beautiful."
She said, "Three is an awkward number."
She said, "*You* used to tell *me* that *I* was beautiful."
She said, "There will be no cell phones at this dinner table."
She said, "I don't care if your teenaged son is calling you from Nepal."
She said, "You're right, I'm not a mother, so I wouldn't understand."
She said, "I care about you a great deal. But you don't make it easy."
She said, "It felt safer to be friends with you when you were married."
She said, "Our worlds used to fit together so perfectly."
She said, "I hear in grief you get a new address book. Well guess what?
    It's true."
She said, "I predict your husband's death will put you in a bad mood
    for ten years."
She said, "I'll only be sticking around for six."
She said, "I miss the Susan who wrote Thank-You notes."
She said, "I would have done anything for you."
She said, "You would have done anything for me."
She said, "I wanted to be an old lady with you in Paris, but I'll be going
    there with my other girlfriends now."
She said, "My mom used to lock me in the closet and leave me there
    for hours. You kind of remind me of her."
She said, "Watching you all hunched over is a lesson in keeping my
    shoulders back."
She said, "Your life changed. I don't see my place in it."
She said, "Although we go to the same therapist, she's advised me to
    end this friendship."
She said, "I need a break from all this sadness."
She said, "I admit, I liked you better before he died."
She said, "Sorry, but I can only show my courage in your dream."

Puzzle Box

Friends will arrive, friends will disappear.
— Bob Dylan

She was like Genie Land,
twirling behind
a pink velvet curtain
in costume.
She was a private amusement
with Arabesque music
in a girlhood setting.
She was a woman's woman,
a marvel to behold.
Our exchange,
that space between luck
and fate.
She was a serendipitist,
her mission, to initiate
one's soaring.
She was a symbol
of her self-made motto:
 "Friendship Never Ends."
But wake up!
Astonishment
is fickle, charm,
a shapeshifter.
She was a projection
with hidden compartments,
fleeting as stardust.

Possibilitarianism

I didn't know if I could keep moving forward, was ready to collapse and feeling as frozen in time as my dead husband. I shared this with my mom when she called to check in like she always did.

"Say affirmations. See the possibilities. Visualize," she said. "I'm buying you a copy of The Power of Positive Thinking. *It's been a lifesaver for me. You need to go out there and act like everything is going great and it will be great."*

Reframing

Now we tell stories,
file emotions in categories
and yet, how quickly we forget,
muscle memory is encoded, declarative.
This is my narrative, a shelter of sentences
to magnify the gulf between us
where the truth must lie.
The truth must lie.

Zig-Zag Lady

Sometimes I am two people. Johnny is the nice one.
Cash causes all the trouble. They fight.
— J.R. Cash

(1)

I learned from Johnny Cash
that wearing black is never wrong;
wore it long before I was a widow
and expected to.

I learned to live in the mouth of joy
while in the arc of grief,
with a deep belief
in co-existence.

Johnny taught me hope's persistence;
how to perfect a numb,
encumbered smile
while shining, while crumbling.

His was an inner swagger, an open shield
which showed me how to yield
when push came to shove—
to rise above temptation, or pretend to.

I've been a celibate whore,
a wayward monk
and every possible swear word
in between.

"Lean in," Cash would say,
if he were a Buddhist yogi
but he was just
another Christian sinner

and Faith is elastic:
swaying me to the swordfight,
the promise of flickering light
if only I tried harder.

Even as The Man In Black
repelled me
with infidelity and plagiarism—
I pedestalized him,

identified with his redemption
and humanity;
his double message
like a smashed mirror,

rear-view and showing me
how clear and fragmented,
how strong and shattered
I really am.

(2)

I learned from Johnny Cash
that I could love you
like an olde tyme country singer;
conviction-based,

laced with gospels
from his mother's hymn book:
"Where the Soul of Man Never Dies"
"In The Garden"

"When He Reached Down His Hand For Me"
 "Soft and Tenderly"
"In The Sweet Bye and Bye"
"Just As I Am."

But our time was short as Modern Country—
a three-minute feel-good, feel-bad song
overladen with adjectives,
an explosive chorus, a redundant verse.

How I curse myself for turning us into
that sheared, haunting ballad
we would both play out,
forcing you to doubt my integrity.

Perhaps, if you knew
I was a lot like Johnny Cash
—two people in one body, cut in half—
we could hold the ornamental staff

together, balance the right with
the cruel as no one is a fool here
and never far from how
I dreamed us into being.

Half Moon

for Mason

> *I raise my hand and touch the wheel*
> *Of change – Taking time to check the dial.*
> — Yusuf/Cat Stevens

We fled the scene by traveling
there was a liberty
in being separated from our story
we didn't have to talk about it
unless we felt like it, unless
we wanted to

When on the plane, about to
take off or land
we would briefly, lightly touch hands
knowing anything could happen
understanding we'd been left with
only each other

Those mere seconds of contact
would save me
would keep me going.

The Lazarus Phenomenon

You're convinced your dead husband has entered the kitchen.
You're packing snacks for a beach day with your adolescent son.
You're on vacation so you let him eat Goldfish and read *People* magazine.
You're allowing him to curse without having to put quarters in the Swear Jar.
You're hallucinating your dead husband, who appears to be on a mission.
You're aware that reunions can be a struggle for separated families.
You're cringing when he announces a full day of planned adventures.
You're fearless when you say, "We already have other plans."
You're not alarmed when he picks up a chair, throws it across the room.
You're either flat-out numb or not afraid of his anger anymore, or both.
You're reminded of a dual character he once played on *The X Files*.
You're sure it was a Monster-of-the Week story in an episode called *Lazarus*.
You're back to believing that the dead can come to life.
You're thinking of that man in Malaysia who awoke for two hours after
    he died.
You're proud to be able to say to your dead husband, "*I'm* the one in
    charge now."
You're positive he never could listen to anyone when he was alive.
You're learning that homecomings with the deceased rarely have
    happy endings.

Unsettled

A slow learnin'
But you learn to sway.
— John Hiatt

When I was married,
there were times I parked in the driveway,
sat in my car, stared at our house
and thought, Who lives here?
Whose life is that?
as if none of it belonged to me.

My husband would appear,
knock on the window and ask,
"Are you going to come in anytime soon?
Your family is waiting for you."

I was hungry. For what, I did not know.
But then he would show up
and remind me: Real love is medicinal,
has healing properties,
reclaims the empty spaces.

Your Mama is a Nostalgia Queen

After your father died, I drove around and cried in his car while listening to songs he wrote and sang: "The Old Road," "Homeless Love," "Bright Angel."

You left your car behind. I drive around in it, try not to cry while listening to songs you wrote and sang: "Absentee," "Cellophane Skin," "Hitting All the Reds."

I do everything as instructed. Accept the timing. Never answer the phone on the first ring. Get a life (coach). I fail miserably but that stays between me and me.

Eight years later on the ride to your college dorm, you ask: "Are you going to get a dog now?" I stop listening to music with words, get heavily into instrumentalists.

The Last Barstool Date of the Loneliness Prevention Society

And I need you more than want you.
— Jimmy Webb

1.

Take me back to the night we met. The Cinema Bar, German beer, first time alone in that atmosphere since my early twenties. Onstage: a man with a sad guitar, movie star good looks, songs of doom and gloom. The player wasn't you, just someone I knew as a widow.

My husband: gone four years. A parade of stalkers and balladeers tramped through my love-life. I had invited them in, then made an abstinence vow to disallow the wrong fingers from handling me. Was forty nine going on fifteen. It felt like there was no one.

"Sugar Magnolia" was playing on the jukebox when you skulked in. We stared each other down then parsed the lyrics. I could feel your wear and tear, searched your outerwear for sparkles of hope: overcoat, Irish flat cap; that overlap in your two front teeth, like mine, only different.

Wanted to tell you, "I feel Grateful. I feel Dead," but cut out of that bar instead before you could make a move or enable me to find things about you to disapprove of. Wondered if I'd ever see you again.

2.

You're like a hybrid of Mary Ann and Ginger, you messaged me on Facebook. After the official friend request, I scoured your Timeline on a quest for clues, found booze and warm friends at Casa Bianca Pizza Pie, a throwback place with Tiffany lamps and upholstered booths.

Booths were our underpinning. For our first date, you'd promised to deliver me one. *"I'll take you anywhere you want to go,"* you said. I chose Dear John's, a dark bar with the older-woman lighting, got there early, sat there fighting an undiagnosed anxiety disorder. You got there late.

I hated dating, though your style *was* crackling: belt-looped keys to whereabouts unknown, prescription Ray-Bans, same ones my Fairfax Grandpa used to wear. We shared a love of vintage biker jackets. Fondling mine, you said, "Good quality," like a scrawl of graffiti.

Everything was going great until you mentioned your dealer while listening to me ramble on about psychics and healers, messages from beyond, how I talked to my husband's ghost on a regular basis. *Magical Thinking* had both saved me and kept me bound to what was.

3.

My heart was a haunted house. No Trespassing! You were a safe bet, fifty nine and never married. And so we made the rounds to every Westside and Eastside café, bar and diner where we wrangled about drugs, the definition of love, and Socialism.

Now every place we ever went has shut down or become something else. Centanni changed to Double Zero, serves plant-based pizza, bio-dynamic wine. Taix is on the decline, soon to become a smaller version of itself with housing and retail space.

Meshuga 4 Sushi has become Berlin's; Spitfire Grill, traded up for craft beer and "ingredient-driven food." Those loved places all disappear over time. But what happens when a *memory* is scheduled for demolition?

"Wichita Lineman" was our song. You'd play it on Friday nights at the Culver Hotel when I was in the room and listening. I know you learned guitar as a way to get girls, played to show parts of yourself you otherwise couldn't reveal; your heart concealed, at risk.

4.

Take me back to the night you left. We're at Vito and I'm fifty five, clinging to worn-thin comfort: your snap-front Pendleton canyon shirt, that hole in your ear where a ring used to be, the length of your beard, rabbinical. As you glare at enamel saints on a grief-aged neck, toenail polish named "Miss Independent," with nothing left to love about me.

Remember when you said you wanted to be part of a team? I believed you, signed on for being alone together, even if it meant making a deal with myself to live without being touched.

Once, we clutched each other like prey animals. Now I'm as numb and disengaged as Joan Didion in that book. Take a closer look, you'll see, my husband's clothes are still hanging in the closet.

I felt guilty for living, the years, disappeared as contrails. Wanted to kill my husband but he was already dead; blamed you instead for everything you couldn't give me, everything I thought I wanted. Stop rolling your eyes. "I'll take you anywhere you want to go."

SITUATED

Alphabet of Assaults

After you jumped, I knew.
Blood on his hands.
Call him out, my son says.
Delaying, out of fear.
Even in accountable times.
For we both survived until you couldn't.
Going to report him anonymously.
Hadn't realized he touched you too.
I track him on White Pages.
Justice will be served internally.
Kept it secret, afraid we'd be separated.
Look-back window is still open.
My time, closing in.
Not like it was in '75.
Only witness, you.
Perpetrator was someone close.
Question is, how many others?
Really need you here.
Statute of Limitations expires December 31st.
The morning after, we called Van Nuys Police.
Until they asked for his name and we hung up.
Vulnerability hounds me.
Wished I had slipped it in, he said.
Xanax helps me sleep.
You remember how he drugged us?
Zeno watches, halfway to healing.

No Regrets, Coyote

There's a Navajo saying: If you encounter a Coyote on your trail, you must turn back and end your journey.

A few years before meeting Chris, he'd written and performed a one-man-show about this very subject. He completely identified with and embodied Coyote – an irresponsible, mythological character who lived for rule-breaking, adventurous mishaps.

When he turned sixty, there seemed to be a shift in him toward strength and wisdom. He revealed, "I'm not a coyote anymore. I'm a bear now."

He believed it. I was beginning to.
Were we ever wrong.

For Miss Brooklyn

We shared a two-person table in art class,
placed there by the teacher to face
each other. You rarely looked up.
I'd struggle for ideas while watching
your effortless hands, and complain about
my husband who was still alive back then,
ramble on about my many crushes:
Tim Russert, Philip Seymour Hoffman,
Michael Moore—unlikely objects of desire.
You'd cringe, roll your eyes, tune me out.
"You're just saying those things to get attention,"
you'd say, and maybe I was. He had not been giving me
enough. I judged you too and knew you wished
to be sharing a table with your old friend, Nancy.
You went way back with her. You'd acted, she
wrote for TV. "Queen of the Movie of the Week,"
she called herself, but in art class she would sit
for hours, examining pictures of trees.
Then, out of nowhere, she died. It pulled us close
together. You learned that I wasn't joking about
my taste in men. We started walking mornings.
Two years later, my husband was dead. We hit the streets
within days. "I'll help you walk through this,"
you told me, or if you didn't say it, you showed it.
Our many changes did not pull us apart. It's easy to
forget where this started, easy to fold ourselves
into this union of words and steps,
walking and talking about everything, about
nothing. Even when there were no words, we
found them. I could not have walked this
aloneness road without you.

Indoctrinated

I went back to see Clarissa the psychic no less than twenty five times in ten years. She was my go-between, that frayed thread connecting death to life. Until the night she shared that Chris was "hanging out with John Wayne, drinking whiskey, chain-smoking Camel Non-Filters because it was like, 'Who the fuck cares?'"

I told her I didn't want to hear about him anymore, that she was better when the body was still warm. I told her I wanted to know what would happen next.

She set down her worn deck of cards, reached for my hand and said, "It's time for you to rewrite this story—your story—from a joy perspective."

The Flowering Period

I always felt like the backyard was *his* garden. We negotiated. We compromised. I got the front, he got the back. Mine was a drought tolerant, lawn-free, cactus-filled landscape, designed as a love letter to him: Boutin Blue fox tail agave, tangerine Kangaroo Paws, Eremophila, New Zealand flax, Woolly thyme and Sedum spurium Dragon's Blood with a substitute lawn of decomposed granite and sandstone.

It was inspired by the 29 Palms Inn, where we'd stayed, first as a couple and then as a family, every New Year's Eve since 1990. And it was a tiny tribute to what was then called "The Monument," soon to be a National Park, where we'd hike until we got lost, scramble over boulders and hide out in caves.

He was a rock climber, surrounded by muted colors of earth and stone. I was an indoor woman and he brought me outdoors, introduced me to road trips, Joshua trees and the Oasis of Mara. I learned to crave the desert, wanted to integrate its beauty into our daily existence.

That said: *My* garden got some strange looks from passersby, baffled by the unfamiliar. This was fifteen years ago, when succulents were not a trademark of residential Santa Monica the way they are now.

His garden was the opposite of mine. He was never just one way. So it became a mixture of all parts of him, all the places he loved: Mediterranean and lush, with grass and wild trees, requiring a lot of water to thrive. He did throw in a few terrestrials, to balance things out and connect our separate visions.

Many of his plants never bloomed while he was living. They flourished after he died, and continue to, these calm reassurances from *his* world, nature. And how he upheld that world in his every day, his hands deep in the dirt, his face animated with delight at each burgeoning sprout.

A few weeks ago, three pineapple-shaped, turquoise Puya Alpestris popped up unexpectedly. They're native to the Chilean Andes, known as sapphire towers. At nearly five feet tall, they've got barbed spikes and flowers that look like they were made out of plastic. And, well. It seems they're butterfly magnets.

I find unbrokenness in what used to be *his* garden, that which is now ours: it is a place that conveys, again and again, that he is watching over us, bringing natural beauty to his family and, in his absence, reminding us of what he deeply valued, back when he was still alive and blossoming.

Solace is to be found there as we carry on, as we keep growing, without him.

Crying, Waiting, Hoping

Mason was on stage playing Chris' guitar, singing Buddy Holly: *You're the one I love and I think about you all the time.* He stood alongside a giant mounted photo on an artist's easel of his father in the snow, skis on his back, poles in hands, looking up at the summit in reverence.

It was a year to the day since Chris lost his life on a mountain like the one in the picture, buried under twelve feet of snow by an avalanche.

Mason had turned twelve. Our friends at the Ruskin Theatre, where I'd produced Chris' one-man show shortly before he died, had given me the space to invite our creative community of actors, writers and musicians to pay tribute to him.

Chris had taught Mason his first chords of guitar and they used to go to Open Mic nights at The Talking Stick, a coffeehouse around the corner from where we lived. Mason would play cover songs—Johnny Cash, Buddy Holly, Janis Joplin—and Chris would back him. Then Chris would perform his own songs and we'd watch from the audience.

Buddy Holly was our family mascot. When Chris was in his teens and twenties, he looked a lot like Buddy and used to sing Buddy's songs with his college friends at Northwestern. He was even up for the lead in *The Buddy Holly Story.* It came down to the wire between Chris and Gary Busey, who got the part and won the Academy Award. Chris never got over not getting cast as Buddy.

Many years after, Mason discovered Buddy's music and would learn to play all of his songs by age eleven. *Buddy Holly's Greatest Hits* was in the CD player of my car the day Chris died.

After our tribute, Mike Myers and John Ruskin approached me. "We want you to create your own show here," John said. "In the spirit of your family," Mikey added.

They saw it as a continuation of the expressive life and collaboration Chris and I shared during the nearly twenty years of being together. They wanted me to have something that was *mine*, where I could rebuild my world while creating a space for other artists. They said they'd give me one Sunday night a month with free reign to experiment and explore.

Mason named the show after what he'd called me the first time he'd seen me in reading glasses, "Library Girl." He'd become the regular opening act, singing covers as well as original songs he'd begun to compose.

Now, more than one hundred and fifty shows later, Library Girl has welcomed countless poets, writers and singer-songwriters to perform their original work and commune. This has anchored me, filled me, revived me. At a recent event, before the audience was brought in, I walked across the theatre floor and backstage, drawn by the otherworldly sounds of Mason, his partner and love, Hannah, and their friend Alex rehearsing what would be the opening song of the night, The Beach Boys' "Little Bird." We were paying tribute to our dear friend, poet Stevie Kalinich, who had written that song with Dennis Wilson in 1968.

Listening to these three and their exquisite harmonies, I could hear echoes of that first night, Chris' year-mark memorial where my show was born. And I could feel reverberations of those treasured times when Chris and Mason would perform at The Talking Stick together.

From the beginning, my hope for Library Girl was that it would stretch time. On this night: It did.

Analog vs. Digital

Any minor world that breaks apart falls together again.
—D. Fagen/W. Becker

My ex-boyfriend Wayne used to tell me that he knew every single time his former wife went crazy. He'd come home and find all the furniture rearranged.

That's what loss did to me. Everything got reconfigured and I didn't have a say in it.

It took a decade to be able to move through the room without tripping over something. Eventually, I found integration and an accidental grace in the rearrangement and I recognized: the real missing person, the one I'd been looking for everywhere, my whole life—was myself.

The Optimistic Widow

for SEH

I believe in fate, fortune tellers, incantations, Marie Laveau, Mary Worth and messages from beyond. I look for signs, I look for signals, wear amulets, protection saints, medals of honor, keep good luck charms in the bottom of my purse and in the pockets of my jeans.

He believes in science, credibility, proven theories from reliable sources. He collects facts, statistics, trivia. Has an encyclopedic memory. Knows the answer (or backstory) to almost everything.

In the summer of 2018, I was healing from a break-up and struggling with a lingering sadness. My mom bought me rose-colored glasses. She promised they would help change my perspective.

I was wearing them when I walked into that restaurant where he was sitting, while we awaited a mutual friend. It wasn't a fix-up and I wasn't interested, but within forty five minutes, I was smash-bang smitten and everything aligned.

I asked him, "Are we the same person?" We'd made the same tracks. We were a widow and widower, having each spent nearly two decades with charismatic adventurers we'd coupled with that same summer of 1990. When they died, we both felt we'd lost our greatest.

This story begins in 1978 at The Shrine Auditorium at a Grateful Dead concert. He and I figured out *that* was the first time we were in the same room together. And we decided, there must have been a thousand more shows over a forty year time span, where we were in the same venue unknowingly.

We were, we are kindred. Besides having the exact initials down to the middle name, our fathers both grew up on the West Side of Chicago. I was on the same spoken word CD as his late wife. And we each lived in Spanish homes built in 1927, with the same four numbers in the address. Even though he doesn't believe in synchronicity, *he's* the one who pointed all of these things out to me.

I didn't want to fall in love with him. I had learned how to take care of me. I'd found an autonomy I'd never known, and every man I'd ever loved was starting to appear in my consciousness as a series of sepia-toned photo strips, a set of exposures.

But it's hard to resist the impulse to capture joy when it's been stolen from your everyday life, as it was for the two of us. Together, we live with the unasked-for knowledge that *who* you count on *most* can just as easily disappear. And yet, we can't think about that every second. We must make it incidental music.

He is more logical than I am and we don't always see things the same way. He didn't attribute the rose-colored glasses with bringing us together, but I did, in part. After we became an official couple, I lost them. I longed to wear them again, but soon realized I didn't need them anymore.

Then yesterday, I was cleaning out my car and saw that they'd been safely hidden for nearly four years in the storage compartment between the two front seats. They've been our unknowing lucky charm, a talisman that has traveled with us, protected us and brought new eyes to a magical thinker and an information seeker.

We are not identical but even with our differences, we are a miracle. He doesn't have to believe in kismet. He understands the marriage of love and grief.

The Bundle Keeper

It was an icy path, the kind I swore I'd never walk again.
It was 4th of July but there had been snow.
It was a pilgrimage, like the Camino de Santiago or Route 66.
It was full of strangers heading in the same direction.
It was mostly unpaved, but concrete in places.
It was like trudging on the side of a highway.
It was Arizona to New Mexico with my son and new husband.
It was all-encompassing and we were determined.
It was time travel as my son was eleven, not the young man he is now.
It was exhausting but we had to move forward.
It was finding what matters most, what matters least.
It was jarring when my new husband told us he forgot his cell phone.
It was he who started walking back to Arizona to retrieve it.
It was just me and my son, just us again, but not for long.
It was my former husband, dead a dozen years, who came to greet us.
It was Who invited you back? and Why'd you ever leave us in the first place?
It was he who sidled up and started ambling alongside us.
It was he who pointed out the fire dance across the highway, the pit of
    glowing embers.
It was hard not to stare at the people who were spinning, twirling, fire
    eating.
It was as if they were half human, half Pac-Man.
It was my momentary wish to join in the dance, be computerized, be
    ancient.
It was my eyes that veered toward my new husband, in the distance,
    returning.
It was my old husband who forged ahead, sensing he was no longer
    welcome.
It was necessary to allow him to walk on, by himself, and not look back.

About the Author

Susan Hayden is a poet, playwright. novelist and essayist. Her plays have been performed on KPFK's Pacifica Performance Showcase and produced at the MET Theatre, Padua Playwrights, The Lost Studio and elsewhere. Her poems and stories have been published in numerous journals and anthologies including Beat Not Beat (Moon Tide Press), The Black Body (Seven Stories Press) and in the bestselling Los Angeles In the 1970s/ Weird Scenes Inside the Goldmine (Rare Bird Books). She was a Top 100 Finalist in the Inaugural Amazon Breakthrough Novel Award with Penguin Press for her unpublished novel, Cat Stevens Saved My Life. Hayden is the creator and producer of Library Girl, a monthly literary series now in its 14th year at Ruskin Group Theatre. In 2015, she was presented with the Bruria Finkel/Artist in the Community Award by the Santa Monica Arts Foundation. She is the proud mother of singer-songwriter Mason Summit, who performs with Irene Greene in the angsty Americana duo, The Prickly Pair. She lives in Santa Monica, California with her husband, music journalist Steve Hochman. Now You Are a Missing Person is her first published book.

Acknowledgments

Thank you to the Editors of the following journals, anthologies, blogs and podcasts for selecting, publishing and/or presenting my work. Many of these pieces appeared in different forms.

"Borrowing Sugar": first appeared on *LK Thayer's The Juice Bar Blog, 2014*; published in the anthology, *Los Angeles In The 1970s: Weird Scenes Inside the Goldmine, Rare Bird Books, 2015*. (Editor: David Kukoff) and in *Cultural Weekly 2015* (Poetry Editor: Alexis Rhone Fancher).

"1971 Was a Bad Year For Certain People": *Cultural Weekly 2020* (Poetry Editor: Alexis Rhone Fancher).

"The Soul Section": published in the anthology, *The Black Body, Seven Stories Press, 2009*. (Editor: Nana-Ama Danquah).

"I Wanted Him": *Edgar Allan Poet Journal #3– Los Angeles Edition, Edgar & Lenore's Publishing House, 2015*. (Editors: Apryl Skies and Danny Baker)

"Her Life as a Sad Country Love Song": featured on Michael Nicolas Delgado's podcast, *A.G. Geiger Presents: Tales from the LA Art Underworld/ #49: Love Letter to LA from Her Top Poets*. The pre-recorded poem was accompanied by original music written and performed by John McDuffie.

"Wormhole," "Butterfly and Moth," and "Darby Slick Was on to Something" are excerpts from the story "City of Rocks": *Angel's Flight literary west (aflwmag.com) - Time, UNREAL March, 2017* (Co-Founders: Michele Raphael and David Lott)

"John Muir Warned You This Could Happen": FINALIST in MacQueen's Quinterly Triple-Q Challenge, published in Issue 11 of *MacQueen's Quinterly, January, 2022. (*Editor: Clare MacQueen)

"Paris 2003" and "Meteorology" (formerly "Full of Life: A Thanksgiving Poem")*: The Examiner* article, Los Angeles Poet Susan Hayden Speaks on Love, Loss and Poetry as Medicine, *June 2010* by Yvonne de la Vega.

"Boys Without Fathers": *Beatnik Ghosts Anthology, Vol. 2, Issue 1*, June, 2011. (Editor: Daniel Yaryan) and Yaryan's *Sparring With Beatnik Ghosts Omnibus Deluxe Edition 2022.*

"Souvenirs and Evidence," "Zig-Zag Lady" (and some of the fragments, previously contained in one poem called "Polavision"): *TribeLA* Magazine 2017. (Article Editor: Linda J. Albertano) and on *LK Thayer's The Juice Bar Blog, 2016.*

"She said, 'The Healing Meter Has Expired.'": published in the anthology *Beat Not Beat, Moon Tide Press, September 2022.* (Editors: Rich Ferguson, S.A. Griffin, Alexis Rhone Fancher and Kim Shuck.) Also presented as a YouTube poetry video in *Plants, Painting and Poetry: Poetry Films, 10/21.* Created and produced by Nicelle Davis.

"The Last Barstool Date of the Loneliness Prevention Society": *MacQueen's Quinterly/ Issue 13. May 2022.* (Editor: Clare MacQueen).

"The Optimistic Widow": title borrowed from a short film by Oliver Rosenfield about my emergence from grief.

"The Bundle Keeper": published within the article, Valentine's Day Redux: a Second Chance at True Love. *Cultural Weekly,* February, 2021. (Selected by Alexis Rhone Fancher, Poetry Editor). Re-published February 2022 in the same publication (now *Cultural Daily*). Also in *Scenes of Southern California: A Directory of So Cal Poets, Four Feathers Press, April 2022.* (Editor: Don Kingfisher Campbell).

Never-Ending Love and Gratitude

to my beloved son
Mason Summit Allport

to my husband
Steve Hochman

to my mother
Vivian Weiss

In memory of
Christopher Allport
(1947-2008)

and

Kimberly Laine Pauli
(1962-2004)

Immeasurable thanks to my closest, most cherished friends and family
(you know who you are)

and to the open-hearted, welcoming literary community
of Los Angeles.

Heartfelt Appreciation for Making this Happen:

Eric Morago of **Moon Tide Press** for seeing something he was
drawn to in an early draft and asking if he could publish this book.
Jerry Garcia for generously connecting us.
Bianca Stone for her exceptional editor's eye and rare insight.
Amber West for the intro.
Cassandra Lane for her brilliant overview.
Tracy Veal for her ingeniousness.
Alyssia Gonzalez and Michele Raphael for getting the word out.
Hazel Angell for their cover art, which became my muse.
Rick Bursky for cleaning up my act.

Also Available from Moon Tide Press

Paradise Anonymous, Oriana Ivy (2023)
Maze Mouth, Brian Sonia-Wallace (2023)
Tangled by Blood, Rebecca Evans (2023)
Kissing the Wound, J.D. Isip (2023)
Feed It to the River, Terhi K. Cherry (2022)
Beat Not Beat: An Anthology of California Poets Screwing on the Beat and Post-Beat Tradition (2022)
When There Are Nine: Poems Celebrating the Life an Achievements of Ruth Bader Ginsburg (2022)
The Knife Thrower's Daughter, Terri Niccum (2022)
2 Revere Place, Aruni Wijesinghe (2022)
Here Go the Knives, Kelsey Bryan-Zwick (2022)
Trumpets in the Sky, Jerry Garcia (2022)
Threnody, Donna Hilbert (2022)
A Burning Lake of Paper Suns, Ellen Webre (2021)
Instructions for an Animal Body, Kelly Gray (2021)
Head *V* Heart: New & Selected Poems, Rob Sturma (2021)
Sh!t Men Say to Me: A Poetry Anthology in Response to Toxic Masculinity (2021)
Flower Grand First, Gustavo Hernandez (2021)
Everything is Radiant Between the Hates, Rich Ferguson (2020)
When the Pain Starts: Poetry as Sequential Art, Alan Passman (2020)
This Place Could Be Haunted If I Didn't Believe in Love, Lincoln McElwee (2020)
Impossible Thirst, Kathryn de Lancellotti (2020)
Lullabies for End Times, Jennifer Bradpiece (2020)
Crabgrass World, Robin Axworthy (2020)
Contortionist Tongue, Dania Ayah Alkhouli (2020)
The only thing that makes sense is to grow, Scott Ferry (2020)
Dead Letter Box, Terri Niccum (2019)
Tea and Subtitles: Selected Poems 1999-2019, Michael Miller (2019)
At the Table of the Unknown, Alexandra Umlas (2019)
The Book of Rabbits, Vince Trimboli (2019)
Everything I Write Is a Love Song to the World, David McIntire (2019)
Letters to the Leader, HanaLena Fennel (2019)
Darwin's Garden, Lee Rossi (2019)
Dark Ink: A Poetry Anthology Inspired by Horror (2018)
Drop and Dazzle, Peggy Dobreer (2018)
Junkie Wife, Alexis Rhone Fancher (2018)
The Moon, My Lover, My Mother, & the Dog, Daniel McGinn (2018)

Lullaby of Teeth: An Anthology of Southern California Poetry (2017)
Angels in Seven, Michael Miller (2016)
A Likely Story, Robbi Nester (2014)
Embers on the Stairs, Ruth Bavetta (2014)
The Green of Sunset, John Brantingham (2013)
The Savagery of Bone, Timothy Matthew Perez (2013)
The Silence of Doorways, Sharon Venezio (2013)
Cosmos: An Anthology of Southern California Poetry (2012)
Straws and Shadows, Irena Praitis (2012)
In the Lake of Your Bones, Peggy Dobreer (2012)
I Was Building Up to Something, Susan Davis (2011)
Hopeless Cases, Michael Kramer (2011)
One World, Gail Newman (2011)
What We Ache For, Eric Morago (2010)
Now and Then, Lee Mallory (2009)
Pop Art: An Anthology of Southern California Poetry (2009)
In the Heaven of Never Before, Carine Topal (2008)
A Wild Region, Kate Buckley (2008)
Carving in Bone: An Anthology of Orange County Poetry (2007)
Kindness from a Dark God, Ben Trigg (2007)
A Thin Strand of Lights, Ricki Mandeville (2006)
Sleepyhead Assassins, Mindy Nettifee (2006)
Tide Pools: An Anthology of Orange County Poetry (2006)
Lost American Nights: Lyrics & Poems, Michael Ubaldini (2006)

Patrons

Moon Tide Press would like to thank the following people for their support in helping publish the finest poetry from the Southern California region. To sign up as a patron, visit www.moontidepress.com or send an email to publisher@moontidepress.com.

Anonymous
Robin Axworthy
Conner Brenner
Nicole Connolly
Bill Cushing
Susan Davis
Kristen Baum DeBeasi
Peggy Dobreer
Kate Gale
Dennis Gowans
Alexis Rhone Fancher
HanaLena Fennel
Half Off Books & Brad T. Cox
Donna Hilbert
Jim & Vicky Hoggatt
Michael Kramer
Ron Koertge & Bianca Richards
Gary Jacobelly
Ray & Christi Lacoste
Jeffery Lewis
Zachary & Tammy Locklin
Lincoln McElwee
David McIntire
José Enrique Medina
Michael Miller & Rachanee Srisavasdi
Michelle & Robert Miller
Ronny & Richard Morago
Terri Niccum
Andrew November
Jeremy Ra
Luke & Mia Salazar
Jennifer Smith
Roger Sponder
Andrew Turner
Rex Wilder
Mariano Zaro
Wes Bryan Zwick

Made in the USA
Columbia, SC
24 May 2023

17118178R00098